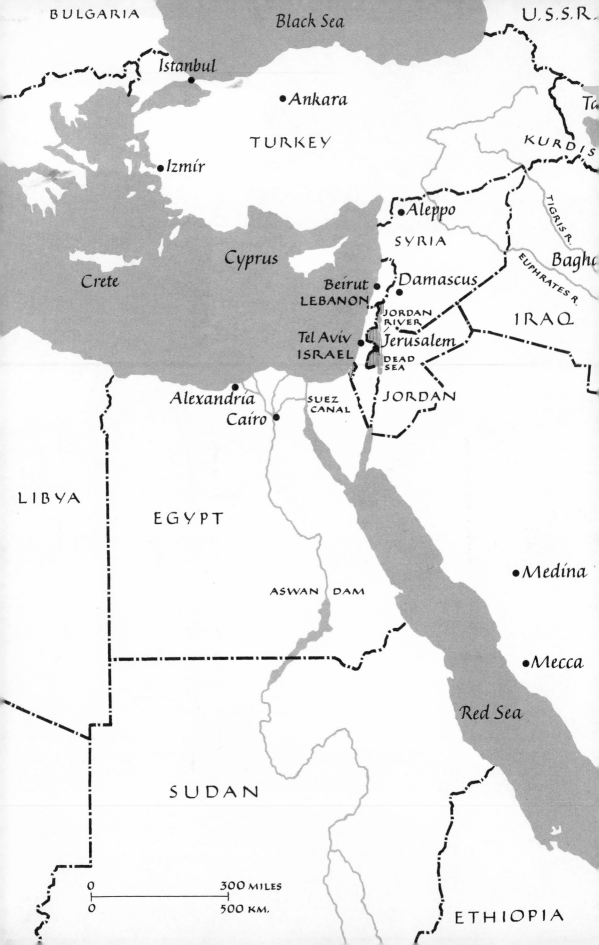

U.S.S.R.

Caspian Sea

•Tehran

Isfahan •   IRAN   AFGHANISTAN

Abadan   PAKISTAN
ra•
KUWAIT

Persian Gulf   STR. OF HORMUZ
BAHRAIN   Gulf of Oman
        Sharjah•
        QATAR
Riyadh•   UNITED   •Muscat
        ARAB
        EMIRATES   OMAN
SAUDI

ARABIA

RUB AL KHALI

SOUTH YEMEN
RTH
MEN   Indian Ocean

• Aden

error and betrayal

IN

LEBANON

An analysis of Israel's invasion of Lebanon
and the implications for U.S.-Israeli relations

GEORGE W. BALL

with a preface by Professor Stanley Hoffmann

FOUNDATION FOR MIDDLE EAST PEACE

1984

Copyright © 1984 by Foundation for Middle East Peace.
All rights reserved.
Printed in the United States of America.

Library of Congress Catalog Number 84-82206
Library of Congress Cataloging in Publications Data
Error and Betrayal in Lebanon:
An analysis of Israel's invasion of Lebanon
and the implications for U.S.-Israeli relations
Ball, George W.
Foreword by Merle Thorpe, Jr.
Preface by Stanley Hoffmann
ISBN 0-9613707-1-8

FOUNDATION FOR MIDDLE EAST PEACE
1522 K Street, N.W., Suite 202, Washington, D.C. 20005

Acknowledgements

I AM GRATEFUL to Mr. Merle Thorpe, Jr. for his wise counsel and editorial advice and to the Foundation for Middle East Peace for undertaking the publication of this book.

I also acknowledge my great indebtedness for the invaluable help and advice of Dr. Douglas B. Ball, Lt. Col., MSC (USAR) who is collaborating with me on a forthcoming book on US-Israeli relations to be called *The Passionate Attachment*.

Several friends have read this manuscript and made useful suggestions, for which I extend my silent thanks. I shall refrain from naming them to avoid associating them with the views I express.

George W. Ball

Princeton, New Jersey
August 10, 1984

Contents

PART ONE: The Invasion and Its Aftermath

The First Phase (June 1982-September 1982)

THE ADMINISTRATION COLLABORATES WITH THE ISRAELIS TO
ACCOMPLISH ISRAEL'S FIRST OBJECTIVE: THE EXPULSION OF THE
PLO LEADERS FROM LEBANON AND THE DEMORALIZATION OF THE
PALESTINIANS.

The Second Phase (October 1982-May 1983)

AMERICA TRIES TO HELP ISRAEL ACHIEVE ITS SECOND SET OF
OBJECTIVES: A FRIENDLY LEBANON UNDER ISRAELI INFLUENCE, A
PEACE TREATY, AND THE EXPULSION FROM LEBANON OF THE
SYRIAN ARMY.

The Third Phase (June 1983-February 1984)

FAILING TO ACHIEVE THE PEACE TREATY IT WANTED AND FINDING
THE GEMAYAL GOVERNMENT TOO WEAK AN INSTRUMENT TO
SERVE ITS OBJECTIVES, ISRAEL ABANDONS ITS GRAND DESIGN,
WITHDRAWING THE IDF TO SOUTHERN LEBANON AND THUS
LEAVING OUR MARINES EXPOSED TO FIRE. ALTHOUGH THIS
DESTROYS ANY CHANCE TO ACHIEVE A UNITED LEBANON FREE
FROM FOREIGN TROOPS, THE ADMINISTRATION STILL PERSISTS IN
PURSUING THAT WILL-O'-THE-WISP.

PART TWO: Lessons and Consequences

Foreword

TO THOSE INTERESTED IN A PEACEFUL RESOLUTION of the Israeli-Palestinian conflict, with security for Israel, the events of recent years have brought only disappointment. The Begin government, while honoring its Camp David commitment to evacuate the Sinai, did not respect its companion commitment to address "the legitimate rights of the Palestinian people". What Israel has actually offered Palestinians, says Amos Elon, noted Israeli author and journalist, is "even less than the South Africans have accorded to their Bantustans".

It is now widely acknowledged that, having neutralized Egypt, Israel undertook its invasion of Lebanon in 1982 to destroy the Palestinian national movement and to remove any barrier to its absorption of the occupied West Bank and Gaza Strip into a biblical "Greater Israel" — this despite the fact that 97% of the population of these territories is Palestinian and despite the overwhelming world view that the territories are the logical place for a Palestinian homeland. Furthermore, it has been pointed out by Ze'ev Schiff, military correspondent of Israel's most prestigious daily, *Ha'aretz,* that "It was sheer folly to believe that any action [in Lebanon] would ameliorate the political conflict between the Israeli and the Palestinian nations."

After analyzing the invasion and the U.S. role in it and its aftermath, George Ball tells us where present Israeli and U.S. policies will likely lead. His grim picture is one on which Americans and friends of Israel would do well to reflect.

George Ball has, during a half century of involvement in foreign affairs, shown a remarkable ability to penetrate prevailing myth and conventional wisdom and identify American interests. As Undersecretary of State during the Kennedy and Johnson Administrations (1961-1966), he opposed America's involvement in Vietnam with persistence and eloquence against strongly contrary views of his colleagues. In recent years he has written extensively on America's Middle East predicament, questioning the indiscriminate U.S. acceptance of Israeli policy as compatible with U.S. interests. Repeatedly he has urged America to develop a coherent policy of its own in that strategic area.

15

Ball has written several books on foreign policy. His recent memoirs, *The Past Has Another Pattern,* were highly regarded. His book on U.S.-Israeli relations, to be titled *The Passionate Attachment,* will be published next year by W. W. Norton & Co.

Professor Stanley Hoffmann has long been recognized as one of America's most distinguished experts on international affairs. Professor of Government at Harvard University for more than two decades, holder of the Douglas Dillon Chair in the Civilization of France, and Chairman of the Harvard Center for European Studies since 1969, he also has written frequently on the Middle East conflict and is the author of many influential books on foreign policy.

Merle Thorpe, Jr., *President*
Foundation for Middle East Peace

Washington, D.C.
September, 1984

Preface

GEORGE BALL'S BLUNT AND DEVASTATING ESSAY is a book of enormous importance. It performs two services for which his readers must be grateful.

The first one is the detailed and incisive demonstration of the fiasco of President Reagan's policy in the Middle East. Commentators have been surprisingly gentle with Reagan's way of handling foreign affairs. They have hesitated to say that the Emperor has no clothes. An ideology entirely devoted to the "restoration" of American strength in the expectation that strength would bring peace and quiet, and to the establishment of a worldwide anti-Soviet "strategic consensus" simply has no formula for coping with the intractable realities; it has been obliged to improvise uncomfortably and, in most instances, unsuccessfully.

Concerning the Arab-Israeli conflict there have been three completely different policies in three years and each one has failed, as George Ball shows. The attempt of General Haig to build a "strategic consensus" led to almost immediate trouble both with the Begin government and with Saudi Arabia; and it led Haig to acquiesce, in effect — by failing to try to prevent and to stop it — in the disastrous Israeli invasion of Lebanon in June 1982. As George Ball points out, Israel's failure to reach all of General Sharon's military objectives resulted from Syria's resistance, not from America's pressure as some myth-makers now suggest. But, partly because of the indignation and pressures of America's Arab friends, the Reagan Administration, after Haig's ouster, made some appeals to Israel to lift the seige of Beirut and sent a force to supervise a partial Israeli withdrawal and the safe exit of the PLO. Next came the episode of the Reagan plan, a classical case of mismanagement, since the U.S. did practically nothing to create the conditions that might have made it possible for the PLO to give a mandate for negotiations to Jordan, and for King Hussein to play the part Washington had assigned to him. Obviously, the Administration decided that the domestic and external costs of putting pressure on Israel were unacceptable.

The third policy — getting a "solution" for Lebanon through a treaty between Israel and the Gemayel government, the exit of all foreign forces from Lebanon, and the consolidation of that government—is an extraordinary example of impossible as well as contradictory objectives and inadequate means. Having inexplicably ignored Syria, the Administration oscillated later between fighting and accommodating Assad, chose to do neither, and was obliged to limit its policy to the protection of its peace force in Lebanon—whose situation had become untenable after Israel's abrupt withdrawal and the resumption of the Lebanese civil war. An undignified American withdrawal marked the collapse of Reagan's last policy in the area.

All of this is documented and analyzed by a man who has no taste for understatements and no respect for fig leaves. But he performs an even more important service by raising fundamental questions about the future. The most upsetting question goes far beyond the Middle East. As Ball puts it, the U.S., in Lebanon repeated the mistake of Vietnam: "the belief that, with resolute will and vast resources, America could mix in the internal affairs of a small country with exotic customs and values and effectively impose a *papier-mâché* regime on all the warring factions." The error of "committing our power and prestige to support a weak government in a local conflict" is being repeated now in El Salvador.

Insofar as the Arab-Israeli conflict is concerned, George Ball's extremely gloomy—indeed, scary—projections must be taken seriously. The dangers of a Middle Eastern Armageddon are real. The great merit of Ball's unflinching analysis is his critique of the American-Israeli relationship, which has had the effect of subsidizing policies that are not in America's long term interest and which undermine the position, in Israel, of all those who want a solution of the Palestinian problem that would allow Israelis and Palestinians to live in peace. Israel, say many of its unconditional supporters in the U.S., is a major "strategic asset" of the U.S. Ball shows why this is not the case—and certainly the Israeli government has repeatedly refused to behave as an American asset.

Even—indeed, especially—Israel's most passionate American friends should read carefully Ball's analysis of Israel's drive for a military alliance with the United States, his description of the risk Israel runs of facing superior Arab forces in the future even if Egypt remains neutral, his demonstration of the disastrous effects of providing a formal security guarantee to Israel as long as it remains at war with most of the Arab countries, and his description of the consequences of allowing Israel, or the pro-Israel lobby in the U.S., to exert a veto on American arms sales to those countries.

Ball's demonstrations and recommendations will undoubtedly be denounced once more as anti-Israel. Obviously, his condemnation of the policies of Begin and Sharon is scathing, and his criticism of the pro-Israeli lobby in the U.S. is fierce. But he harbors no illusons about the Arabs' diplomacy and "failure to face reality" or to help the Palestinians. The remarks he makes about the effects of Israel's move, and of America's support, are those one hears in Israel, where the many groups that seek peace and security ask with despair how much longer the U.S. will in fact pay for and encourage an Israeli policy that leads every day more and more obviously to a *de facto* annexation of the occupied territories, and will turn Israel into a state in which, as in South Africa, discrimination is institutionalized, and more than a third of the inhabitants are deprived of the rights available to the majority. "The adoption of hegemony instead of coexistence" is neither in the long term interest of Israel nor in that of the U.S. There is nothing "anti-Israel" about condemning a course that leads either to the major confrontations Ball foresees or to the corruption of the Zionist ideals and of Israel.

George Ball says little about an alternative course, although his demolition of past American policies suggests what it ought to be. The search for a negotiated solution of the Palestinian problem, based on the two principles of Palestinian self-determination *and* security for Israel, requires the participation of both the U.S. and Israel. As long as the U.S. does not make clear, by the use of its enormous leverage, that it wants Israel to give up its present policy and to negotiate the end of occupation, the momentum of annexation will continue and the forces for peace will, in Israel, remain a bitter minority. Conversely, America's pressure has a chance of succeeding only if it pushes Israel further in a direction in which a sizable fraction of the Israeli public and political establishment wants to go. At this point this seems to be the case in Israel—although it is far from certain that this fraction will prevail. But it will not prevail or be strong enough to make and to impose the drastic changes that are needed if it gets no support from Washington (pressure can be a form of support). In Israel at least there is an open, searching, searing debate. In the U.S., beyond the idiocies of the election campaign, there is nothing: neither debate nor policy. Hence the importance of Ball's masterful essay.

Stanley Hoffmann

Cambridge, Massachusetts
July, 1984

MIDDLE EAST

CYPRUS

Aleppo

SYRIA

Beirut

Damascus

LEBANON

Mediterranean Sea

JORDAN RIVER

Tel Aviv

Jerusalem

Amman

DEAD
SEA

ISRAEL

JORDAN

Alexandria

SUEZ
CANAL

Cairo

SAUDI ARABI

EGYPT

Red Sea

162 км.
100 мı.

Introduction

OUR FIASCO IN LEBANON recalls an old nursery rhyme that I first heard nearly seventy years ago, and which beguiled English children long before that.

> *The good old Duke of York,*
> *He had ten thousand men.*
> *He marched them up to the top of the hill*
> *And he marched them down again.*

As many will recall, the old Duke of York, who was the second eldest son of George the Third, was not regarded in his day as very bright. But there was still much to be said for him. He knew when he marched up the hill why he was going there, and he recognized when he got to the top that he was in an untenable situation so he marched his troops back down again. Finally, when he reached the bottom, he knew where he had been and why he had gone there.

It is too bad that the old Duke was not available to advise us on a policy for Lebanon. Our government could have profited from his wisdom.

THE CENTRAL QUESTION

How did the United States get involved in Lebanon?

The answer is shamefully simple. Since the Reagan Administration lacked any coherent Middle East policy of its own it supported, without critical sensitivity, the policies, decisions and actions of the Israeli government, apparently unaware of the fact that Israel's objectives in Lebanon diverged sharply from America's. By failing to assert our nation's rights, enforce its laws and protect its interests, the Administration encouraged Israel in an adventure that was ill-conceived and disastrous for both countries. Then, even after the Israeli government had abandoned that enterprise as unachievable, the Administration continued to pursue it to the point of inevitable failure.

The episode provides a case study in how not to conduct foreign policy. I have divided the study into two parts. Part One describes the Israeli invasion and its aftermath. Part Two assesses the consequences of our involvement in Lebanon and suggests the lessons to be drawn from that experience, particularly with respect to our relations with Israel.

WHY WE FAILED

UNTIL 1982 THE UNITED STATES HAD AVOIDED INVOLVEMENT in the Lebanese civil conflicts that had raged intermittently for almost a decade.[1] Unlike the Arab-Israeli struggle and the Iran-Iraq War, Lebanon's internecine squabbling posed no substantial threat to our interests in the Middle East. Lebanon possesses no significant military power and is not a menace to its neighbors; it produces no important raw materials, as do the states of the Persian Gulf. For America, it has only marginal political, military or economic importance.

The Reagan Administration did not deliberately decide to involve us in Lebanon. The actions that led us on our aberrant course were not planned or directed from Washington but from Jerusalem and the American government seemed largely unaware of Israel's far-reaching motives for attacking Lebanon in June 1982 or for the implications or even the timing of that attack. For almost a year Israel had been enjoying far more tranquility on its northern border than it had for a long while. The PLO in Lebanon had — at least temporarily — stopped harassing Galilee and was substantially observing a cease-fire which America had helped arrange in July 1981. Syrian President Hafez al Assad was out of favor with much of the Arab world because, in the course of his feud with fellow Baathists in Iraq, he had closed Iraq's pipeline through Syria and was supporting the Khomeini regime in the Iran-Iraq War. Although Syria was receiving limited arms from the Soviets, Russia had no effective presence in the area. As a nation friendly to both sides in the Arab-Israeli dispute, America was continuing to try — as it had done for many years — to play a mediating role in an effort to promote progress toward a solution of the long-festering Palestinian problem.

That was the situation when Israel began its invasion in June 1982. As a result of events set in motion by that invasion and by America's mindless response to it, our country lost almost three hundred marines dead, while 1800 were entrapped for seventeen months in an indefensible position and exposed to fire. For more than 22 months in the waters off Lebanon we maintained a huge fleet manned by 30,000 sailors and carrying 100 planes on constant alert against kamikaze attack. We used the guns and planes of that fleet to kill an unknown number of Druse, Shiite and Syrian soldiers and civilians. When we finally withdrew at the end of the day we had paid a high price in the hard currency of our dignity and our reputation for sound, common sense. We had accomplished nothing. We had actively participated on the losing side of a neighborhood quarrel that was none of our business; we had wasted valuable time that should have been devoted to resolving the Palestinian issue and, from the point of view of both Israel and the United States, had left the situation materially worse than before. As a result of Israel's attack, Syria received over $2 billion of arms from the Soviet Union as well as intensive Soviet military instruction and, by calling up reserves, it increased its army to 400,000 men. Thus, not only have the Soviets acquired a far greater military presence in the Middle East (at least 12,000 military personnel) but Syria now poses a much more critical threat to Israel.

None of that would have happened had the Administration clearly defined America's proper objectives in the Middle East and acted incisively to advance those objectives. But that would have meant dealing firmly with Israel and no American administration has done that since the days of President Eisenhower; instead, throughout the Lebanese episode, Washington flaccidly let the Begin government, in effect, dictate America's policies and disregard America's interests. Such apparent impotence reflected an upside-down relationship unique in history. Although Israel is, in practical terms, a ward of the United States—dependent on America for economic, financial and military support to a degree without parallel between sovereign nations—the United States is more often the suppliant than the dominant partner.[2]

In the second part of this book I shall discuss the political conditioning that has produced this extraordinary state of affairs; meanwhile it is sufficient to note that the phenomenon does not arise from lack of potential leverage but from a paralysis of the political will. Thus the President and the Congress have unquestionable power, as President Eisenhower demonstrated, to assure that Israel's policies and practices are consistent with American objectives—and indeed they are obligated by their oaths of office to make sure that America's resources are not used to harm our interests—yet they are prevented from utilizing that leverage by crippling domestic constraints.

Paralyzed by domestic pressures, our government does not even require that Israel keep its explicit contract commitments and obey the same rules we enforce on other nations. Under the U.S.-Israel Mutual Defense Assistance Agreement of 1952, Israel formally committed itself to use the military equipment we provide *"solely* to maintain its internal security, its legitimate self-defense or to permit it to participate in the defense of the area of which it is a part or in United Nations Collective Security Agreements and measures, and that it will not undertake any act of aggression."

Two American laws provide for the enforcement of that agreement.[3] The most relevant is the Arms Export Control Act, which provides that, whenever the President finds that a purchaser of arms under the agreement may have violated those conditions of use, he must promptly report that information to Congress. When the President finds that a violation has occurred, or Congress makes a similar determination by joint resolution, the offending country will be ineligible for any credits or guarantees, as well as cash sales and deliveries under previous sales. When Turkey violated a similar commitment by using American-supplied military equipment to invade Cyprus in 1974, the United States strictly enforced the law, suspending all military assistance for two years, even though Turkey was a member of the NATO Alliance and the Cypriote Government had provided substantial provocation for the invasion.[4]

But our political leaders habitually treat Israel as exempt from normal rules. Not since 1956 has any American government subjected, or even convincingly threatened to subject, Israel to any significant sanctions for flouting its commitments.[5] Although some military shipments have been briefly held up, the Israelis never take our gentle gestures seriously, since they know that, with the mobilization of their political troops in Washington, they can easily overcome the obstruction. Thus threats of sanctions have become a meaningless minuet. To enforce the penalty provisions in contracts would, according to Israel's apologists, violate a sacred taboo; it would be "putting pressure" on Israel.

But is that an accurate formulation of the issue? The President and the Congress are obligated to spend American taxpayers' money frugally to advance American policies and secure its interests. How then can they justify using that money to provide weapons and economic aid that Israel uses to pursue military expeditions and occupation practices that frustrate our policies and damage our interests? That is an overriding issue of principle; the contract restrictions Israel has accepted as a condition to receiving our aid are merely applications of that principle.[6]

ISRAEL'S TWO OBJECTIVES

POLITICIANS EAGER FOR VOTES incessantly refer to Israel as "America's most dependable ally in the Middle East." But is there any subtance in that phrase? As this book will make clear Israel has followed a pattern of conduct quite inconsistent with that of an ally. It has repeatedly begun major military adventures without prior notice to our government, sometimes practicing deception to conceal its plans. Even when it has advised Washington of impending military operations, it has several times misrepresented its true intentions and its true objectives. Nor has it paid much attention to our requests for restraint.

That was certainly true when Israel invaded Lebanon in June 1982. Then the Begin government sought to achieve two objectives which it concealed both from the American government and the Israeli people. Had Israel's public been honestly informed of what was being undertaken—and particularly had it anticipated the casualties involved —I doubt that a majority of Israelis would have approved the full scope and purpose of the invasion General Sharon was launching. What is clear beyond question is that his objective severely cut across America's interests.

Sharon's first objective related not to Lebanon so much as the West Bank, which the current government passionately claims as a part of Eretz Yisrael ("The Land of Israel"). Even before Begin's Likud Party came to power, Israel had already begun the tactic of trying to foreclose—or at least circumscribe—any negotiated solution of the West Bank problem by preempting the land and water supply through the establishment of settlements at key points in the area so as to create "new facts." The tactic of the Begin Government—which it made little effort to conceal—was to stay rigorously away from the bargaining table until it had settled so many Israeli citizens on the West Bank as to absorb the whole territory, in fact if not in law. Meanwhile the 900,000 Palestinians in the West Bank would face the dismal choice of either living under conditions approaching apartheid or moving to other parts of the Arab world—particularly to Jordan.

In Israel in 1979 I talked with General Sharon who, as Minister of Agriculture, was then in charge of the settlements program. When he told me of his plan to settle a million Israelis in the West Bank within the next 30 years, I asked him if that meant that the government planned to push out the Palestinians who lived there, forcing them to resettle in Jordan or some other Arab country. He turned his back and walked away. According to a friend of mine, Sharon later responded to the same question with the sardonic comment: "Oh, we'll keep enough for labor."

The major obstacle to Sharon's scheme was the continued existence of the PLO, which the great majority of Palestinians—including those in the West Bank—recognized as their exclusive spokesmen. To remove that obstacle Israel's hardline strategists were determined to destroy the PLO not merely as a military but—much more important—as a political force. That required that the PLO be "decapitated"—a winsome formulation which meant that its leaders must be either killed or dispersed throughout the Arab world. The strategists were not seriously concerned at the PLO's military power—Israel possesses thirty times the military force that the PLO could possibly improvise. Nor did all of them really want the PLO to stop its terrorist activities. Extremists in the government found those activities politically useful, since they served to dehumanize the PLO and, by association, all Palestinians—to make them appear to the world as, to use Prime Minister Begin's words, "beasts walking on two legs."[7]

Thus, according to a leading Israeli scholar, Yehoshua Porath, the Begin Government was annoyed when, during the latter part of 1981 and the early part of 1982, the PLO continued to observe the cease-fire that Ambassador Philip Habib had arranged. If the PLO could achieve such discipline, it could in time develop a respectability that would force Israel to serious political negotiations. As a result, Porath wrote,

> "the Government's hope is that the stricken PLO, lacking a logistic and territorial base, will return to its earlier terrorism: it will carry out bombings throughout the world, hijack airplanes and murder many Israelis. In this way, the PLO will lose part of the political legitimacy that it has gained and will mobilize the large majority of the Israeli nation in hatred and disgust against it, undercutting the danger that events will develop among the Palestinians that they might become a legitimate negotiating partner for future political accommodations."[8]

By destroying the PLO as a political force, the Begin government hoped to gain a free hand to impose its will on the leaderless West Bank Palestinians, while restricting the concept of Palestinian "autonomy" to the supervision of such routine tasks as street-cleaning and garbage collection and totally ignoring Palestinian "self-determination." In fact it hoped to destroy the PLO so completely that, in the words of one of Israel's senior diplomats, "they (the PLO) are dead people politically."[9] At the same time at least some hardline elements favored measures to create such demoralization as to deter the Diaspora Palestinians from interfering. Indeed there is evidence that those elements in the government even hoped that, with their Phalange collaborators, they could spread such terror in the refugee camps of Lebanon as to goad the

Palestinians into panic-stricken flight to Syria, following the tactic of the Deir Yassin massacre in 1948.[10]

General Sharon was convinced that "quiet on the West Bank" required "the destruction of the PLO in Lebanon."[11] As Yoel Marcus wrote in *Ha'aretz*, "behind the official excuse of 'we shall not tolerate shelling or terrorist actions' lies a strategic view which holds that the physical annihilation of the PLO has to be achieved. That is, not only must its fingers and hands in the West Bank be amputated (as is now being done with an iron fist), but its heart and head in Beirut must be dealt with. As Israel does not want the PLO as a partner for talks or as an interlocutor for any solution in the West Bank, the supporters of confrontation with the PLO hold that the logical continuation of the struggle with the PLO in the occupied territories is in Lebanon."[12] So Israel invaded Lebanon with the thought, as the then Foreign Minister (now Prime Minister) Shamir put it, that "the defense of the West Bank starts in West Beirut."

Israel's second objective in launching the invasion related more to Lebanon than the occupied areas. Although the Reagan Administration seemed unaware of it, General Sharon was pursuing a geopolitical scheme that reflected an ambition of key Zionist leaders even before the creation of the State of Israel. To Zionist geopoliticians, Lebanon was the "detachable weak link" that could break up the anti-Israel Arab front, and the Maronite Christian element in Lebanon was the vehicle for achieving such a "detachment." The grand old man of Israel's early history, David Ben-Gurion, wrote in his diary on May 24, 1948:

"the weak link in the Arab coalition is Lebanon. Moslem rule is artificial and easy to undermine. A Christian state must be established whose southern border will be the Litani. We shall sign a treaty with it."

Then, on June 11th, three weeks later, he wrote: "in the Galilee, the main enemy is [sic] Lebanon and Syria and our aim is to hit Beirut and to rouse the Christians [to revolt] . . ."[13]

Six years later Ben-Gurion was still advocating this strategic scheme. On February 27, 1954, Prime Minister Moshe Sharett, described in his own diary Ben-Gurion's frantic advocacy of that objective.

"This is the time [Ben-Gurion said] to push Lebanon, that is the Maronites in that country, to proclaim a Christian state. . . . He began to enumerate the historical justification for a restricted Christian Lebanon. If such a development were to take place, the Christian powers would not dare oppose it!"

Sharett, who opposed the plan, then injected the comment that ". . . if we were to push and encourage it on our own we would get ourselves into an adventure that will place shame on us." Nevertheless, proponents of the scheme continued to agitate for it and contacts were apparently made with some Lebanese circles. Then, on May 16th, Ben-Gurion further outlined his scheme at a meeting where Moshe Dayan was present. Again, as recorded by Prime Minister Sharett, Dayan said:

> ". . . the only thing that's necessary is to find an officer, even just a major. We should either win his heart or buy him with money, to make him agree to declare himself the saviour of the Maronite population. Then the Israeli army will enter Lebanon, will occupy the necessary territory, and will create a Christian regime which will ally itself with Israel. The territory from the Litani southward will be totally annexed to Israel and everything will be all right."

Later on May 15th, Prime Minister Sharett's diary notes: "the Chief of Staff supports a plan to hire a [Lebanese] officer who will agree to serve as a puppet so that the Israeli army may appear as responding to his appeal to liberate Lebanon from its Moslem oppressors. This will of course be a crazy adventure. . . ."

When planning began for the Sinai-Suez operation of 1956, the Lebanon plan was put on the back burner. But it was revived after the Yom Kippur War of 1973, and this time the Israelis obtained their puppet Maronite major—Sa'ad Haddad, an officer in the Lebanese army, who, in 1979, declared a Maronite state in southern Lebanon. This was the first step in a strategy that was elaborated during repeated visits between members of the Israeli government and Bashir Gemayel.

Bashir was the son of a prominent Maronite Christian leader, Pierre Gemayel, who had founded a political party with an attached private army, the Phalange, which he had named for General Franco's forces and patterned after Hitler's Brown Shirts. Succeeding his father "as the military and political leader of the Phalange," Bashir "enjoyed unimpeachable authority." Israel maintained close relations with the Phalange through agents of a government agency roughly equivalent to the American CIA called the MOSSAD (the Institute for Intelligence and Special Assignments). Israel guaranteed the security of the Phalange and provided it with arms, uniforms and training.[14]

American correspondents on the spot were aware of the intrigue. *Time*, on February 15, 1982, reported that in mid-January General Sharon had flown to meet Bashir Gemayel aboard an Israeli gunboat off the Lebanese coast to discuss how Israel and the Phalange would cooperate in a planned invasion that would, so *Time* stated, "bring Israeli forces as far north as the edge of Beirut International Airport."[15]

The grand design agreed between Israeli's strategists and the Phalange was fatally flawed by arrogance, insensitivity, and a naive belief in the universal efficacy of military force. The IDF would invade Lebanon and link up with the Phalange; then, with the leverage provided by the IDF's presence, the Phalange would install Bashir as President of Lebanon. After establishing a government friendly to Israel and amenable to Israeli influence, Bashir would, on behalf of that government, sign a formal treaty of peace. That treaty would, they hoped, satisfy two Israeli ambitions. It would by its terms accord Israel full diplomatic relations—a step that would advance Israel's strategic plan to settle with one Arab neighbor at a time—and, in addition, it would provide Israel effective control of Southern Lebanon—thus assuring it both additional territory and an effective buffer zone.[16]

Finally, once the new Lebanese government was firmly established Israel would assist it in expelling the Syrians from Lebanon and extending Gemayel's control throughout the balance of the country. Thus, the execution of the plan would put Israel in position to influence, if not dominate, its northern neighbor.[17]

General Sharon's apocalyptic vision was even more spacious. Israel, he and his colleagues planned, would do everything possible to induce West Bank Palestinians—and, with the help of the Phalange, other Palestinians in Lebanon—to take refuge in Jordan where their burgeoning majority would force the overthrow of the Hashemite 'dynasty. That, Sharon hoped, would generate such chaos as to justify Israel in intervening, and ultimately, dominating, Jordan. The result, so he and his friends saw it, would be to extend Israel's hegemony all the way to Saudi Arabia, thus making it the overwhelming master of the Middle East. At that point, Sharon believed, one Arab country after another would sue for peace.[18]

Of course, such opium dreams did not represent an accepted stategy even for the Begin Government, but how far was that Government fully in command of Sharon and his Napoleonic ambitions? So long as he seemed to be winning, the Cabinet seemed quite prepared to ratify his actions—no matter how much those actions may have caught the ministers off balance.

Meanwhile the Reagan Administration continued to demonstrate a respectful innocence and, without understanding why and how it was letting itself be used, became a passive accomplice in at least the first chapters of this madly ambitious scheme. As a result, America was led, step by faltering step, into a humiliating and costly enterprise.

PART ONE

The Invasion and
Its Aftermath

THE FIRST PHASE

(June 1982-September 1982)

THE ADMINISTRATION COLLABORATES WITH THE ISRAELIS TO ACCOMPLISH ISRAEL'S FIRST OBJECTIVE: THE EXPULSION OF THE PLO LEADERS FROM LEBANON AND THE DEMORALIZATION OF THE PALESTINIANS.

Israel Begins its Invasion

DURING 1981 ISRAEL INITIATED A SUCCESSION OF MILITARY ACTIONS that took our government by surprise. On June 7, 1981, it used eight F-16 jet fighter bombers escorted by six F-15s to destroy Iraq's nuclear reactor. That action was an act of war, in clear violation of international law (think of the outcry had Iraq attacked Israel's Dimona reactor!), and it exposed the technical secrets of some of the United States' most sophisticated weapons to possible compromise had one of the planes flamed out or otherwise fallen into Iraqi hands. Yet President Reagan's only comment was that Israel may have sincerely believed the raid was a defensive action, adding, "It is very difficult for me to envision Israel as being a threat to its neighbors."[19] Prime Minister Begin, who had timed the attack to help his electoral campaign, immediately used those words in election rallies to prove that President Reagan supported Begin's hardline policy.

On July 17 and 18, 1981, the Israelis again used planes we had supplied to bomb apartment areas of Beirut on the asserted excuse of knocking out a PLO headquarters. Those raids killed over 100 and wounded some 600, most of whom were civilians. Although that action was clearly not "legitimate self-defense" under any reasonable definition of the term, President Reagan did not raise that embarrassing point. Instead, he directed his special Middle East envoy, Philip Habib, to negotiate a cease-fire binding on both Israel and the PLO. That cease-fire became effective July 24, 1981, and survived an extraordinary series of provocations.

On December 14, 1981, Israel formally annexed the Golan Heights, which it had seized from Syria in the 1967 war. Although the United States voted for a United Nations Security Council Resolution calling Israel's annexation "illegal" and threatening "appropriate measures" unless it were rescinded, Israel treated these admonitory words with the shrug they deserved. Its leaders knew the American Government would do nothing to enforce them,[20] and they were quite right; only four months later, on April 25, 1982, when Israel finally completed its withdrawal from the Sinai as agreed at Camp David, the Senate Foreign Relations Committee voted to increase America's grant aid to Israel by $350 million.

In view of such a pattern of complaisant behavior the Begin government had good reason to believe that Washington would not interpose
serious obstacles in the event the Israel Defense Forces (the IDF)
should move across the Lebanese border. It had particular confidence
in the tacit support of Secretary of State Haig. When he had first visited
the Middle East in the Spring of 1981 he had, in the words of two
informed Israeli correspondents, "left his hosts with the distinct impression that America intended to take a hard line toward Syria as the
Soviet Union's chief client state in the region,"[21] and throughout the
events that preceded and followed the invasion Haig consistently
supported Israel against more critical voices in the Reagan Administration, including Secretary of Defense Weinberger.

Unlike the situation at the time of Israel's Suez attack in 1956, our
government was certainly not taken by surprise when the IDF moved
into Lebanon. It had plenty of advance notice during which it might
have planned an appropriate response. In October 1981, when Secretary of State Haig met Prime Minister Begin at President Sadat's
funeral, Begin told him, so Haig records in his memoirs,[22] "that Israel
had begun planning a move into Lebanon and would not draw Syria
into the conflict." Haig responded with what was to become his ritual
reply: "If you move, you move alone. Unless there is a major,
internationally recognized provocation, the United States will not
support such an action."

That, according to Haig, was only the beginning, for "in the months
ahead, the subject would arise again and again." While Haig repeatedly
emphasized that "the United States would never tell Israel not to
defend herself from attack" he still insisted that "any action she took
must be in response to an internationally recognized provocation, and
the response must be proportionate to that provocation."

Not only did the Administration know that Israel planned to invade
Lebanon; it had clear notice well in advance that the IDF would push
as far as Lebanon's capital. On February 3rd, Haig writes, Begin sent
the director of Israeli military intelligence to tell him that Israel was
prepared to dispatch a large-scale force "from the Israeli border to the
southern suburbs of Beirut" with its target "the PLO infrastructure",
adding that "the Syrians would be avoided if possible." Haig also notes
that he knew of Sharon's visit to his Phalangist allies in Beirut. "Soon
afterward," Haig admits, *The New York Times* carried a remarkably
detailed account of the Israeli plan. It was no longer much of a secret;
nor was it any secret that time was running out," for, late in May,
"General Sharon shocked a room full of State Department bureaucrats
by sketching out two possible military campaigns: one that would

pacify southern Lebanon, and a second that would rewrite the political map of Beirut in favor of the Christian Phalange." Haig claims to have challenged those plans, warning Sharon with the by then stylized cautionary words that, without an "internationally recognized provocation," an Israeli invasion of Lebanon "would have a devastating effect on the United States." Sharon's answer was equally stylized: "no one has the right to tell Israel what decision it should take in defense of its people."

Later, when faced with overwhelming evidence of an imminent, Israeli attack, Haig wrote Begin on May 28, 1982, that he "hoped there was no ambiguity on the extent of our concern about possible future Israeli military actions in Lebanon. . . . Israeli military actions, regardless of size, could have consequences none of us could foresee." Once again Begin replied in his established idiom: "Mr. Secretary, my dear friend, the man has not yet been born who will ever obtain from me consent to let Jews be killed by a bloodthirsty enemy and allow those who are responsible for the shedding of this blood to enjoy immunity."

On reading these words Haig writes that he "understood that the United States would probably not be able to stop Israel from attacking," which meant, in other words, that he would not try. Although he admits that he "never believed that mere words would restrain Israel," he did not go beyond cautionary abstractions. Not once did he suggest to Begin that the penalty for using United States equipment in such an attack might be the suspension of further military aid. Indeed, there is considerable evidence to suggest that Haig never really wanted to deter the Begin government from carrying out Sharon's "grand design." In the words of two respected Israeli jounalists, Ze'ev Schiff and Ehud Ya'ari, ". . . Israel could not have asked for a better spokesman for its cause than Secretary of State Alexander Haig. Washington—unsolicited, it seemed—was going to do its part by protecting Israel's political flank, giving Menachem Begin good reason to feel that he was standing on solid ground."[23]

Haig was not alone in thinking that "time was running out," for Sharon was acutely aware that the Lebanese elections were scheduled to be held on August 23rd and that the IDF had to be in Beirut to make certain that Lebanese democracy worked as Israel decreed and that Bashir Gemayel was installed as President. Thus, Israel's search for an "internationally recognized provocation" became increasingly frenetic. On April 21, in ostensible retaliation for the killing of an Israeli officer by a land-mine in Lebanon, Israel's air force bombed suspected PLO positions in Lebanon killing 23 persons. On May 9, following the attack on a bus in Jersualem, Begin formally renounced the cease-fire agreement, and the Israeli Air force bombarded what were alleged to be PLO headquarters, killing 11 and wounding 56, very few of whom were in any way connected with the PLO.[24] Unable to stand down indefinitely, the PLO finally felt forced to respond by firing 100 rounds of Katyusha rockets into Israel. On May 15, the Israeli Army Chief of Staff, General Rafael Eitan, confirmed that 30,000 troops were massed along the Lebanese border.

All these noises off stage were a mere curtain-raiser for the long-awaited main event. On June 4, 1982, a terrorist splinter group obligingly furnished Israel at least a shadowy *casus belli* by wounding an Israeli envoy in London. Although British Government investigators announced that the attack was not the work of the PLO but of a radical anti-Arafat group headed by Abu Nidal whose hit list included PLO leaders, that did not matter to Prime Minister Begin. In fact, far from being one of Arafat's agents, Abu Nidal was Arafat's most bitter enemy on whom Arafat had pronounced a death sentence, yet Eitan angrily dismissed such a fastidious distinction. "Abu Nidal, Abu Shmidal" he is reported to have said, "we have to strike at the PLO."[25] As he and his colleagues saw it, Palestinians were fungible; such groups, so Israel's then Ambassador to Washington (later Minister of Defense) Moshe Arens commented, were "all of the same mafia-type octopus that works out of Lebanon."*

> The Israeli reaction resembled that of the overly diligent policeman engaged in breaking up an open-air Communist rally in Boston. When one bystander pleaded, "Don't hit me, I'm an anti-Communist!" he was answered by a sharp blow on the head and the angry comment: "I don't care what kind of a damned Communist you are. You can't meet in this park!"

In any event the London shooting gave the Israelis their long-awaited "provocation," although one might still doubt that it was "internationally recognized" as Haig had prescribed. But for the Israeli armed forces D-Day had now arrived. Within hours waves of Israeli jets struck PLO villages and centers on the Lebanese coast, finally goading reluctant PLO leaders into responding with artillery fire along the frontier. On June 6, 1982, the IDF pushed north across the Lebanese border.

The Israeli government had timed its initiative in accordance with its established practice. As usual it sought to catch the world—and particularly the United States—off guard. It had launched its invasion of the Sinai on October 31, 1956, at the moment when statesmen were preoccupied with the Soviets' bloody repression of Hungary, and only days before the American Presidential election on November 6th. Then, on December 14, 1981, just when world attention was focused on the declaration of marital law in Poland and the arrest of the Solidarity leaders, it had precipitately annexed the Golan Heights. This time the Israelis timed their invasion of Lebanon to coincide with the Falkland Island crisis and the attendance of President Reagan and Secretary Haig at a summit conference in Versailles.

Once the attack had begun on June 6th, the United States supported a United Nations Security Council resolution demanding a cease-fire which Israel promptly rejected. Two days later, while Haig was with the President in Windsor Castle, William Clark, the President's National Security Advisor, gave him a note; it advised him, so Haig writes, "that a resolution had been introduced in the UN condemning Israel for its invasion and threatening sanctions" and it suggested that the United States might vote in favor of the resolution. That "would have been an unprecedented step for the United States," writes Haig, apparently unaware of the actions of the Eisenhower Administration twenty-six years before. It would, he writes, have been "entirely out of character for the President."[26]

Since the resolution was about to come to a vote in New York, Haig acted quickly and, even though Clark assured him that the President had decided to support the resolution "on the basis of a recommendation from the Vice President's Crisis Management Team," Haig told the President "that the United States must veto the resolution not only because it placed the entire blame for hostility on Israel, but also because sanctions were implied. If the United States took this step against Israel, then it must be prepared to take the next, much more serious, step." When Haig's advocacy prevailed and the President agreed to a veto, Haig recites, in breathless, heroic prose, that, "With only minutes to spare, I telephoned Mrs. Kirkpatrick and instructed her to veto the resolution, regardless of any other instructions she may have received, whether or not Israel was named in the resolution."

Still the shadow-play continued. On June 9th the President appealed to Begin to accept a cease-fire and on June 10th a similar message was sent through Ambassador Habib to President Assad of Syria. Assad expressed interest in a cease-fire but only in connection with unconditional Israeli withdrawal, while Begin rejected a cease-fire "until Israeli objectives had been achieved." Later on that same day Haig discovered that the President "had already signed a letter to Begin calling in harsh terms for an unconditional Israeli withdrawal from Lebanon." Clark, so Haig writes, "had engineered," the letter, but Haig quickly intervened to block it.

By June 13th the IDF had closed the ring around Beirut; the invasion, so Haig writes, "had become an Israeli-Syrian war and, now, the siege of an Arab capital."[27]

Haig's account of his activities during the period leaves ample scope for speculation. Although he made cautionary noises in advance of Israel's initial invasion, he concedes that he knew they would have no deterrent effect. At the same time he acted frenetically to block his colleagues in the government from committing the Administration to support effective Security Council action against Israel, then intervened to save the Israeli government from a Presidential scolding. The fact that Israel, using weapons we had provided it for self-defense, had invaded Lebanon, gratuitously attacked Syrian forces, and was ravaging Beirut seems to have concerned him not at all.

The most plausible inference from Haig's activities and inactivities is that he was basically sympathetic even with Sharon's larger plans. Haig had said in a speech on May 28th—less than two weeks before the invasion began when he must have known Sharon's intentions—that "the time has come to take concerted action in support of both Lebanon's territorial integrity within its internationally recognized borders and a strong central government capable of promoting a free, open, democratic and traditionally pluralistic society." He seems thus to have believed Sharon's contention that, by creating a Maronite Christian government dominated by Israel, the Israelis could create "a strong central government" and force out the Syrians. If so, he revealed a lamentable ignorance of Middle Eastern realities coupled with an inability to recognize that a "pluralistic [Lebanese] society" was utterly incompatible with an Israeli-imposed Maronite domination of the country, which is what Sharon was seeking.

2

Israel's Army Keeps Advancing

THAT THERE WERE DIVIDED VIEWS WITHIN THE ADMINISTRATION seems obvious, but, even so, Haig's position seems remarkably incoherent. Why did he insist that the United States use its veto in the Security Council to save Israel from the international censure of an action which he had—so he says—strongly advised the Israelis not to take? An even larger question is, of course, why the Reagan Administration meekly ignored so many broken promises without bringing Israel up short. Even though Haig makes clear that the Israeli Prime Minister knew better, Begin still assured the President more than once that if an

invasion occurred, the IDF would push no farther than a line 40 kilometers (25 miles) from the Israeli border in order to put Israeli territory
out of reach of Palestinian artillery. He also gave assurances that Israel
would not attack Syria unless its forces were fired upon, and that Israel
did not intend to seize any Lebanese territory.[28]

Begin showed almost total trust in American gullibility—and with
good reason—for Israel's larger ambitions were already in the public
domain.[29] For example, on April 8, 1982, in an NBC television report,
John Chancellor had accurately described Israeli intentions in what,
according to the distinguished Israeli defense correspondent Ze'ev
Schiff, "amounted to a virtual exposure of the Israeli war plans,"
including the plans for attacking Beirut and confronting the Syrian
forces in the Beka'a Valley. Schiff offers convincing evidence that,
contrary to subsequent pretense, Washington was "duly informed"
about Sharon's plans "that went beyond southern Lebanon."[30]

Yet no attempt was made to hold Israel to its word. Instead, the
Administration reversed the position it had taken in supporting the
first Security Council resolution, which had demanded a cease-fire on
the first day of the invasion. Now it was using the soft language of
Caspar Milquetoast, expressing "regret at the spiral of violence that
began with the assassination attempt against the Israeli ambassador."
(Thus implicitly taking seriously what was a hollow pretext). Israel, our
government lamely said, "will have to withdraw its forces from Lebanon,
and the Palestinians will have to stop using Lebanon as a launching pad
for attacks on Israel," but that pious whisper was drowned out by the
noise of bombs and gunfire as the IDF continued its attack. No
American official seriously suggested that, if Israel continued to misuse
the weapons we had provided in violation of its contract commitments,
our government might apply the penalties provided by law. The administration did not even threaten to rescind its recent offer to sell Israel
an additional 75 F-16 fighter aircraft.[31]

Comment:

It was one thing for the Israelis to try to push the PLO far enough above
the border (25 miles) to put their artillery out of range of Galilee, but
their march to Beirut was quite a different matter. Although the Israelis
had suffered but few casualties from Lebanon for almost eleven months
there was evidence that the PLO was moving additional guns into the
area and thus a limited operation might conceivably have been considered as "legitimate self-defense."

But to push all the way to Beirut, attacking Syria en route could not
be considered "legitimate self-defense" without making total nonsense

of that phrase; indeed, even Israeli casuists referred to the war as Israel's first "war of choice," or, in other words, the first war Israel had fought that was *not* for self-defense.[32]

In such a situation our response should have been as prompt and firm as when the United States Government suspended all military assistance after Turkey had used our weapons in invading Cyprus. Those sanctions had been put into effect on February 5, 1975. On July 10, 1975, the future Secretary of State, Cyrus R. Vance, and I jointly testified before the International Relations Committee of the House of Representatives to support the continuance of the sanctions even though some argued that they were impeding a negotiated solution to the problem. We jointly told the Committee that while the United States had been pumping an inordinate amount of arms particularly into the Middle East "our one safeguard is that most of these arms are provided under express conditions that they will be used only for the purposes for which they are explicitly provided, which are solely for internal security, legitimate self-defense, and to permit the recipient country to participate in collective security arrangements. . . . But that raises the central question: How can we preserve the credibility of these conditions if we are prepared to ignore them in the case of Turkey in a highly visible situation which all the world is watching?"

Secretary Vance and I were concerned, as we stated, that any compromise on the issue "would create a widespread impression that no nation that has acquired arms from the United States need any longer pay attention to the conditions on which those arms were made available but would be free to use them in pursuit of its own interests in local conflicts." Our advice to the Committee was clear: Turkey should not be granted discriminatory treatment; it should be held to the letter and spirit of the law. Since that view was shared by a majority in Congress, arms shipments to Turkey were held up for a full two years.

Our comments regarding Turkey applied even more emphatically to Israel, since its invasion of Lebanon was less justified than Turkey's invasion of Cyprus. But the Reagan Administration was guided by what it regarded as the grimy realities of domestic politics rather than the need to apply justice even-handedly or to protect American interests conscientiously. Both the Turkish and Israeli situations involved ethnic lobbies, but, in the two cases, the dominant lobbies were on opposite sides of the issue, and, as is usual in politics, the result depended on whose ox was gored. The Greek lobby demanded that Turkey be subjected to sanctions and, since there was no effective Turkish lobby, sanctions were applied. The Israeli lobby maintained that sanctions should never be applied against Israel, and, since the Arabs were politically ineffective, sanctions were never even threated.

By failing to enforce America's laws and contract rights to stop the IDF from invading Lebanon and letting the IDF use our equipment to kill whoever got in the way, our country became, in the eyes of many, at least a passive accomplice to Israel's aggression. By acquiescing in the brutal excesses of the Begin Government, our government betrayed those moderate, compassionate Israelis who cherished their country's reputation for humanity and were appalled by the sanguinary events unfolding before their eyes. The distinguished military commentator Ze'ev Schiff has described this poignantly missed opportunity.

> A more resolute American response would have strengthened moderate elements in the cabinet and would have prevented the two-month shelling of Beirut. Israeli cabinet ministers who were against extending the war to Beirut said they could not oppose the plans as long as Washington did not come out against them. "I cannot show myself to be less of a patriot than the Americans," one minister said. Later, when the Israeli government was considering plans to enter West Beirut, the same minister said: 'The Americans have got Israel into a mess. They have got us to climb up a high tree and now it's a hell of a job climbing down again.'[33]

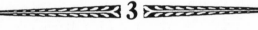 3

Israel Attacks Syria

NOT ONLY DID THE IDF SMASH ITS WAY TO BEIRUT in violation of assurances it had given, it quite gratuitously attacked Syria's forces in eastern Lebanon. Syrian troops had been there ever since 1976, when the Christian-dominated Lebanese government had invited Syria to move forces into the Beka'a Valley to help control the PLO and Moslem elements that were then on the point of defeating the Christians.

Syria clearly did not want war with Israel, and, as Israeli military commentators have made clear, General Sharon did not need to attack Syria's forces to clear the twenty-five mile zone that was the government's announced objective. However, Sharon made a clash with the Syrians inevitable when, the very day (June 8) the Cabinet communique dictated by Begin announced that the Syrians would not be attacked if they did not fire first, Sharon sent a column up the central axis through the Chouf Mountains to the Beirut-Damascus highway with the intention of outflanking most of the Syrian forces in Lebanon. Those forces were under orders to attack any Palestinians or Syrians they might encounter. Begin applauded the move as a tactical masterpiece.[34] An arrogant and vindictive act, it may have caught at least some of the Israeli cabinet by surprise, since, on June 6, the day the IDF crossed the Lebanese border, the Cabinet had declared that "during the operation, the Syrian Army will not be attacked unless it attacks our forces." Once again Israeli action taken without notice to our government had undercut American diplomacy. Indeed, Washington was made to look increasingly foolish. On June 7th Haig told the Washington press corps that the State Department had sent a message to Assad repeating Israel's reassuring statement. That presumably meant that he really believed that the IDF intended to avoid a clash with Syria; otherwise, as Schiff and Ya'ari point out, "he wouldn't have troubled his officials in Washington and the American embassy in Damascus to serve as Menachem Begin's messenger boys."[35] Not only did Haig swallow the Israeli line but he induced the President on June 9th to send a message to Chairman Brezhnev urging him to use his influence to persuade Syria to accept a cease-fire, and to make strong appeals to both Begin and Assad asking for such a cease-fire. Assad had expressed interest in a cease-fire although only in connection with an unconditional Israeli withdrawal; Begin had flatly rejected such a step until Israel had achieved its objectives. The next day, when Begin telephoned Haig he was, Haig writes, in "voluble form" providing detailed information on the Israeli-Syrian air battle over the Beka'a.[36]

Comment:

Although the IDF deployed four divisions with strong air support and the Syrian air force was out of the battle during most of the period, the IDF still failed to attain its military objective of capturing the Beirut-Damascus Highway. When the cease-fire was declared on Friday, June 11, its columns had not cut the highway in the Syrian sector. Its progress, as is described in the Postscript of this book, was far less than had been anticipated, for the IDF had met unexpectedly effective resistance from Syrian ground forces.

Still it was dramatically successful against the Syrian air force and Syria's air defense, smashing Syria's missile sites and shooting down a large percentage of its air force. That feat of arms was greeted by some thoughtless elements in the Pentagon with momentary gloating as demonstrating the superiority of American weapons. But its long-term effects were extremely costly in both military and political terms. The IDF gratuitously threw away an asset of great value not only for Israel but for America. It provided both the Russians and Syrians with detailed knowledge of their own tactical and technical deficiencies, which they could then correct. It gave away its own brilliantly effective tactics that Israel's armed forces had developed over nine years of concentrated effort ever since the Yom Kippur War, thus enabling the Syrians to devise counter measures. Beyond that it betrayed American secrets, since it revealed to the Russians the precise effectiveness of our sophisticated weaponry, yet, as usual, our government uttered not even a whimper.

If the military costs were painfully great the political costs were even more excessive. By making it evident to the world that America's first-class weapons were superior to the less advanced planes and missiles the Soviets had provided Syria—at least when used by Syria's inadequately trained personnel—the Israelis violated an elementary principle of prudence: they humiliated a super power. Moscow's response was prompt and predictable. It reequipped Syria's forces with advanced Soviet weapons, and since the Soviet high command never entrusts its best equipment for unsupervised use by client states, Moscow sent along 7000 troops to guard them, train the Syrians in their use and even man the missiles based in Syria. For the first time since 1976, when Sadat expelled Soviet advisors from Egypt, the Russians now had a substantial presence in the Middle East with the initial contingent now increased to more than 12,000, manning some of the densest anti-aircraft defenses in the world. By misusing our weapons without notice to us, Israel had altered the power equation in the area to its own and America's disadvantage.

There are indications that several of Begin's ministers were opposed to engaging Syria in direct hostilities, and that, had the United States Government moved incisively to warn Israel against tangling with Syria, we could have counted on significant Israeli support. But once again the Reagan Administration failed America's true friends and strengthened Israel's fanatical expansionists. Responsible, moderate Israelis who prefer peace to everlasting war earnestly looked for some signal of support from the United States, but none was forthcoming.

Israel Ravages West Beirut

SENSITIVE TO THE IMPLICATIONS AND CONSEQUENCES, Israel's leaders had, over the years, as a matter of settled practice, refrained from

sending the IDF into an Arab capital. But General Sharon was con-
temptuous of such refined political thinking. At the outset, he moved
his forces up to the gates of President Sarkis's palace at Baabda, then
made a brief incursion into Christian territory at Bahmadoun. Although, for the time being, he kept the IDF outside West Beirut—the
haven of the PLO leaders—that was not for reasons of compassion or
political *delicatesse;* he wished to avoid casualties. As Secretary Haig
has written:

> "... the Israelis had lost 170 killed and 700 wounded thus far ... to capture
> Beirut in street-to-street fighting would have cost many more lives. Ambassa-
> dor Moshe Arens had told me that Israel did not want to go into Beirut and
> pay this price."[37]

Thus to save his own forces, Sharon opted for siege tactics as against
selective killing, using the IDF's most lethal American-made guns,
planes, and naval artillery to subject the heavily settled areas of West
Beirut to a nine-week air, land, and sea bombardment that killed far
more civilians than Palestinian fighters. In addition to thousands of
bombs, some 60,000 shells were fired into the city.[38]

That action critically compromised Israel's standing as a humane
nation. The United Nations Security Council on August 1, 1982,
unanimously "demanded" an immediate cease-fire and asked for the
dispatch of United Nations military observers to assure that it was
maintained. Although the United States voted for the resolution, Israel
with customary scorn rejected any United Nations observers. They
"could," it said, "in no feasible, technical way, monitor the activities of
the terrorist organizations in Beirut and its environs;" instead the
United Nations presence "would signal to the terrorist organizations
that they are not obliged to leave Beirut."

Our government again did nothing to enforce the Security Council
Resolution for which it had voted. Instead the Administration limited
its actions to helping Israel achieve its purpose of expelling the PLO
leaders, thus saving Israel from the formidable casualties and world
condemnation involved in invading West Beirut. It sent Ambassador
Philip Habib to negotiate arrangements for their departure, and, as a
result of his efforts, a ceasefire was established on August 3, which called
for the forces on all sides to hold their positions. But when the PLO
leaders obstinately (or bravely, depending on one's point of view)
refused to comply with General Sharon's *demarche* to leave, Sharon
flouted the cease-fires, intensified the bombardment, and finally moved
the IDF into West Beirut. Since that threatened to wreck Habib's
negotiation it proved too much even for President Reagan. No longer
able to ignore the mounting public outrage, the President, on August

4, called the Israeli assault "a disproportionate" move. In a note to Prime Minister Begin he stated that Israel's actions raised a serious question about whether Israel was using American weapons for "legitimate self defense"—an historic bit of understatement. Israel should, he urged, yield the military gains it had made, return to the ceasefire line of August 3rd, and stop "unnecessary bloodshed." Speaking to a group of 190 American Jewish leaders transported to Jerusalem for appropriate indoctrination, Begin angrily shouted: "Nobody should preach to us. Nobody, nobody is going to bring Israel to her knees. You must have forgotten that the Jews kneel but to God." Since Reagan was not God but only Santa Claus, Israel's cabinet brusquely rejected the President's request to pull its forces back. They would, they said, be kept there as long as the PLO leaders remained in West Beirut.

To make sure that no one underestimated the Begin Government's contempt for America's opinion, a "senior Israeli official" warned on August 6, that any United States pressure on Israel would provoke an "unpredictable" Israeli response. Such an action, the senior official said, "will have a contrary effect and America will lose all of its leverage. Then what Israel will do is unpredictable, but it could make Beirut look like peanuts."[39] The threat was oddly and sadly reminiscent of President Nixon's "madman theory."

As usual the United States turned the other cheek to such Israeli recalcitrance. When, on August 4—the day of Reagan's protest—the United Nations Security Council adopted a new resolution "censuring" Israel for the invasion of West Beirut, America abstained. Instead of serving notice that the continued misuse of America's weapons would be penalized, the President merely asked the Begin government to pause in its destruction of West Beirut long enough for our Ambassador to complete his negotiations to secure the PLO withdrawal that Israel said it wanted. The Israeli government replied with threat and condescension: it might hold back the IDF briefly but not long. Habib would have to hurry, for Israel was "losing patience" and America had better get on with it or Israel would intensify its murderous assault.

Finally, on Wednesday, August 11, 1982, Israel accepted the evacuation plan "in principle" subject to "suggestions for a number of amendments." But the next day, Sharon ordered his air force to mount the most ferocious attack so far; it lasted 11 hours until finally Lebanese authorities felt compelled to suspend the peace talks. As two Israeli correspondents described it:

> 'Black Thursday,' as it came to be known, was a nightmare in which the saturation bombing came on top of a massive artillery barrage that began at dawn and continued throughout the eleven hours of the air raid. Unofficial statistics counted 300 people dead in West Beirut that day.

And, they further commented:

> What made 'Black Thursday' so terrifying was the sense of brute violence run wild, given the sharp contrast between the progress in the negotiations and the savage attack on the city. The wife of Prime Minister Wazzan declared a hunger strike to protest the action, and the Moslem leaders of West Beirut phoned the American embassy with harrowing descriptions of wanton destruction and frantic cries for help.[40]

Since that overstepped even President Reagan's high threshold of tolerance, he telephoned Prime Minister Begin to express his "outrage" (so the White House reported) that the continued Israeli attack would cripple Habib's negotiating effort. Israel's attacks, he said, had caused "needless destruction and bloodshed." But even then no representative of our government threatened to enforce America's contract rights as had been done against Turkey. Indeed, the only threat was a message delivered by the American Ambassador to Israel that if the bombing on August 12 were not stopped, Habib would cease his efforts to negotiate the removal of the PLO leaders.[41]

Comment:

During the whole period of the siege of Beirut the Administration deliberately evaded using its leverage with Israel by refusing to make the finding required by law. Only after the Israelis had for a month fired American shells and dropped American bombs on the residential sections of West Beirut did the President, on August 4, even suggest that such attacks "raised serious questions about whether Israel was using American weapons for legitimate self-defense." Key members of Congress were more incisive; as early as June 21 the late Clement J. Zablocki, Chairman of the House Foreign Affairs Committee, had told reporters after meeting Prime Minister Begin that he was positive that Israel had violated United States law in using American military equipment in the Lebanon invasion. "There is no doubt in my mind," Chairman Zablocki said. "The law is very clear—it is intended for defensive purposes."[42] On July 16, Zablocki complained that the Administration was taking too long to report on the weapons' use; "there is," he said, "no reason to wait six weeks" to make a report. Later in the day the Administration responded by sending a classified report to the Congress acknowledging that Israel *"may have"* violated its legal agreement to use US-supplied weapons only for defensive purposes. The weasel phrase "may have" was the minimum required by law; the Administration carefully refrained from expressing an opinion that would trigger an arms cut-off. It was an obvious evasion of responsibility, a classical example of a timid President passing the buck to an equally timid Congress. As a result some of our country's European friends not only began to shake their heads in wonder but to ask a disturbing question. For all the vaunted virtues of American democracy, how really effective is a political system so paralyzed by domestic pressures that it lets its interests be compromised and its rights and laws flouted by a country only one-fifty-fifth its size?

The Casualties

No one can say with anything approaching precision the number of casualties (mostly civilians) the Israeli army, navy and air force inflicted. The Lebanese Government casualty figures reflect police records which in turn are based on reported actual counts in hospitals, clinics and civil defense centers. On December 21, 1982, in *The Christian Science Monitor,* John Yemma quoted the Lebanese police as stating that between June 4 and August 31, 1982, a period ranging from the first Israeli bombing raids until completion of the Palestinian withdrawal, 19,085 people were killed and 30,302 wounded. In Beirut alone 6,775 died—84% of them civilians—so the police reported. In southern Lebanon, which the Israelis blitzed through in less than two weeks, only 20% of the dead were civilians, the rest were Palestinian, Syrian or Lebanese fighters. Add to that the 328 people known to have been killed and the 991 missing in the massacres at Sabra and Shatilla, and, even if all the figures are overstated by a factor of two, the carnage and wreckage are still ghastly.

Israel has also offered figures for casualties within Lebanon, but they have been ridiculed by reporters and relief workers. There were, the Israelis reported, only 930 people killed in Beirut, including 340 civilians, while the number of PLO killed was given as 4,000. Then, for some unclear reason, the IDF posted in its official spokesman's office outside Beirut a list of casualty figures that indicate that well over 12,000 Lebanese civilians, Syrian soldiers and Palestinian guerrillas were killed.[43] The Israeli army, meanwhile, announced that 446 of its soldiers were killed and 2,383 wounded between June 4 and November 19.[44]

Cluster Bombs

Our laxity in allowing Israel to misuse our advanced aircraft and artillery was bad enough, but the Administration condoned an even more gross abuse when it failed to stop Israel from using cluster bombs in violation of its commitments. The IDF used several different types. One type consists of a cannister containing hundreds of explosive pellets, another type contains a number of small, heavy "bomblets" shaped like arrowheads. In any event, a single bomb containing over

700 bomblets can destroy an area the size of a football field, tearing to bits any human being who may have the bad luck to be within range.

The United States first provided such bombs to Israel during the 1973 Yom Kippur War. Because of their inherently barbarous effects, we made them subject not only to the general law limiting American-supplied weapons to purposes of self-defense, we subjected them to special restrictions. Under an agreement of December 16, 1976 between Israel and the United States, Israel pledged that it would not use cluster bombs unless it were attacked by more than one country and that, even in that case it would use them only "against fortified military targets." Later, under agreements dated April 10th and 11th, 1978, Israel agreed to the additional conditions that it would not use cluster bombs unless *"attacked"* by the *"regular forces of a sovereign nation in which Israel is attacked by two or more of the nations Israel fought in 1967 and 1973."* Additional provisions also prohibited the use of cluster bombs "against any areas where civilians were exposed." The Carter Administration insisted on that last agreement during angry meetings with Israeli officials following CIA reports that Israel had flagrantly violated many restrictions on cluster bombs during its 1978 "Operation Litani." At that time, according to CIA reports, Israel had "saturated South Lebanon with US cluster bombs—mainly against civilian refugee camps."[45]

Against this background one would suppose that the United States would have totally stopped the shipment of such weapons to Israel, but our government continued to supply them. The result was fully predictable. A recently completed 18-month study has now established that, during the invasion of Lebanon, Israel used cluster bombs widely and indiscriminately against civilians. According to a classified CIA report, it used nine types of American cluster bombs in Lebanon, while a further study has disclosed 19 locations in West Beirut as well as 51 named locations throughout Lebanon where Israel used such bombs. While the multinational force was cleaning up explosive fragments, it found more than 3,000 unexpended cluster bomblets, while doctors in the 20 hospitals and clinics operating in West Beirut have signed affidavits regarding their treatment of cluster bomb patients. Cluster bombs were commomly referred to as "the napalm of Lebanon."[46]

In spite of this compelling evidence of wanton misuse, our government, on July 9, only briefly suspended transfer of further cluster bombs to Israel; then, as a part of the so-called Strategic Cooperation Agreement arranged during Prime Minister Shamir's visit to Washington on November 28-29, 1983, President Reagan once again lifted that suspension. The fact that the Pentagon confirmed, on December 6, 1983, that the United States was itself using cluster bombs against

Syrian positions in Lebanon only adds to this sickening recital. We neither enforce the standards we enjoin on others, nor do we set an example by adhering to them ourselves.

5

America Organizes the First Peacekeeping Force

THE IDF LAID SIEGE TO WEST BEIRUT in a classical medieval pattern. In order to bring pressure on the 6000 Palestinian fighters trapped in the city, it began on July 4 to deny food, water and fuel to 500,000 civilians by blocking almost all traffic into the area. In spite of the Reagan Administration request that Israel move its forces back from West Beirut and return to the positions held prior to August 1, the Israelis flatly refused. That adamant stand made it necessary to provide some sort of peacekeeping force to separate the Israeli forces from the PLO leaders and permit the evacuation.

Habib's proposal was to send the Lebanese army into West Beirut to accept the heavy arms of the Palestinians and deploy a United Nations peacekeeping force to guarantee the safe evacuation of the Palestinians. That proposal would presumably have won approval by the Security Council. Soviet President Leonid Brezhnev announced on July 20 that the Soviet Union would support the use of a United Nations force necessary for peacekeeping, but objected to the injection of United States forces into the area.[47] That is an important point to record, since memories are short and it is easy for special-interest partisans to rewrite history. In spite of President Brezhnev's clear statement, President Reagan would later (in February 1984) excuse his Administration's failure to arrange a United Nations solution by claiming that Moscow had blocked his "preference" for a UN force—and that has become a widely accepted story. Isn't Moscow the source of the evil?

Still the President was right on one point: his Administration had preferred a United Nations solution. But it was Israel that vetoed the proposal, not the Soviet Union. According to the report of a House Committee on Armed Services, investigating the security of our Marine contingent, "Ambassador Philip Habib . . . testified that a United Nations force to supervise the withdrawal was not acceptable to Israel. Robert Dillon, the US Ambassador to Lebanon . . . testified that the

Israelis would not trust any international force unless the United States participated."[48]

Most likely, Israel did not want any peacekeeping force at all. In July Israeli officials leaked a story that the President had decided to deploy American forces in a peacekeeping role. Israel's purpose for leaking, some suspected, was to provoke the PLO to reject the plans then still being negotiated, so the IDF could continue its bombardment. In any event, the leak produced repercussions in Washington. The thought of committing Marine units to the Middle East was unpalatable to key members of Congress. The Senate Majority Leader, Senator Howard Baker, remarked that it was "not wise to introduce American fighting men in the Lebanese conflict" and the same sentiment was expressed by Senator Charles Mathias as well as by the Chairman of the House Foreign Affairs Committee, Congressman Clement Zablocki. Nor was the Defense Department favorable. The Secretary of Defense, Caspar Weinberger, warned against sending troops into such a "volatile area." But Israel rejected a United Nations force and that, of course, was the end of it. Under pressure to find a quick solution to halt Israel's brutal bombardment, the President reluctantly agreed to a multinational force with an American contingent.

Once again Israel had its way, in spite of the fact that, as one observer pointed out, never before in modern history had the aggressor been permitted to dictate the form and composition of the peacekeeping force its aggression had made necessary.

Thoughtful Americans were unhappy with the outcome, nor was the risk of American casualties their only consideration. To deploy our forces only 300 miles from the Soviet border (though 5000 miles from the United States) was bound to disturb the Soviets. As might have been expected, Chairman Brezhnev wrote to President Reagan on July 7, threatening that, if the United States sent troops to Lebanon, the Soviet Union would "build its policy with due consideration of that fact."[49] The White House responded with a disdainful dismissal. The Soviet Union also made clear that it would continue to restrict its activities to the resupply of arms lost by the Syrians and the Palestinians and would continue to press for an Israeli withdrawal.

On July 14, the issue of sending troops was still reported to be unsettled. Meanwhile, the Israelis kept threatening to move farther into West Beirut to find and kill the PLO leaders if progress were not made quickly, thus putting the United States negotiators under increasing pressure. On July 17, *The New York Times* reported that two possible roles for the marines were under consideration in Washington and in Middle East capitals. One called for American forces to serve temporarily to guarantee the safe passage of the PLO leaders out of

Lebanon; the other contemplated that the American troops would play the longer-range role of trying to keep apart Israeli and Lebanese forces while encouraging the creation of an effective Lebanese government. Many members of Congress seemed willing to accept the short-range assignment but there was little enthusiasm for maintaining our forces in the country for any extended period. In fact, the Senate Majority Leader, Howard Baker led the chorus of opposition to a long-term peacekeeping role.[50]

On August 15, 1982, the Israeli cabinet finally announced that it had accepted Habib's plan for the deployment of an international peace force in Beirut. On August 29, 1983, the Lebanese Government formally asked the United States, France, the United Kingdom and Italy to send their troops to oversee the evacuation.

Comment:

The role of a peacekeeper should be to interpose its forces between the contending parties and thus stop the fighting; it should not participate in the fighting in any way nor should its forces carry any heavy arms. For obvious reasons that role is appropriate only for nations which have no special interests in the area or special relations with any of the contending parties. That, by definition excludes the superpowers, for the rivalry of the two competing systems plays at least a symbolic part in the policies of almost every area of the world, stimulating and intensifying local passions and jealousies. Thus, as I told the Senate Foreign Relations Committee in testimony at the time: "We would imprudently hazard the lives of our marines to commit them to an area where anti-Americanism is a dominating sentiment." And I added further that, although America might facilitate the removal of the PLO leaders, "there will be plenty of frustrated Palestinians left behind and they may be driven to desperate acts of terrorism by the atmosphere of death and violence that has enveloped the city." If there must be some third party intervention, I proposed: "let the troops of other nations undertake it—young men who are not Americans and hence not the natural targets for assassins."

But the Administration ignored all such cautionary counsels. On August 25, it sent 800 marines into Lebanon to join units from France, Italy and the United Kingdom in a multinational peace-keeping force. Our marines, the President announced, would stay in Lebanon "in no case . . . longer than 30 days," and our commanders were to deploy our Marine force only in areas where there was little danger. Nevertheless the Administration was uneasy about the general situation and it abruptly withdrew the force after only 17 days (August 26-September 11)—a precipitate departure encouraged by Sharon and his colleagues who feared that the peacekeeping force might inhibit their efforts to clear out the PLO Arafat was allegedly leaving behind.[51]

That abrupt withdrawal surprised the other nations that had committed units to the multinational force. It was, as it turned out, tragically premature because our troops left before we made any effective arrangements to assure the safety of the PLO families left behind in the camps.

6

Interlude: President Reagan Puts Forward a Peace Plan for the West Bank

ALTHOUGH MANY ISRAELIS HAD BEEN DEEPLY DISTURBED by the IDF siege and bombardment of West Beirut and particularly by the civilian casualties that resulted, such misgivings were quickly forgotten once the PLO leadership had been evacuated. Prior misgivings were overcome in the euphoric conviction that the invasion had succeeded; in fact the polls showed that 80% of Israel's population now approved of the war.[52]

Several American columnists joined Administration spokesmen in the rejoicing, some suggesting that Israel had done America a great service by driving out the PLO leaders, "liberating Lebanon" and making it possible to get on with the West Bank negotiations. No one seemed to notice that the Begin government had undertaken to smash the PLO infrastructure for the precise purpose of frustrating such negotiations.

The faddish slogan at the time was that the "new realities" of the situation in Lebanon created by the invasion had created "new opportunites" for a fresh start toward a solution of the Palestinian issue. Secretary Haig had been dismissed in July and, in the words of William B. Quandt, who had a major role in Middle East policy under the Carter Administration, "the 'strategic consensus' school was in disrepute and many of its practitioners had been sent packing."[53] The new Secretary, George Shultz, so Quandt wrote, "carried little ideological baggage and was seemingly prepared to take a fresh look at Middle East policy."[54] Thus conditions were ripe for President Reagan on September 1st, to put forward what came to be known as the Reagan Plan.

Two realities and two issues, the President said, provided the context for American policy. The two realities were, first, that the military losses of the PLO had not diminished the need to find a just solution for the Palestinian people, and, second, that Israeli military prowess had not brought that country peace. The two issues were the strategic threat posed by the Soviet Union and its surrogates and the achievement of peace between Israel and its Arab neighbors.

The initial Arab reaction to the President's language was cautious and generally positive. For many Arabs the Reagan Plan seemed to provide a long-missing element; it implied an American recognition that the Palestinian question was the central problem of the Arab-Israeli conflict, even though the President was deliberately ambiguous in using such phrases as "legitimate rights," "full autonomy," "disposition of Jerusalem," "Palestinian-Jordanian entity," and "Israel's final boundaries" and explicitly ruled out the establishment of a Palestinian state. The plan, in Quandt's words, "was noteworthy as much for what it left out as for what it said" since, he pointed out, "Lebanon was briefly mentioned, Syria was not."[55]

But the Begin Government's reaction was emphatically negative. Resolutely determined to avoid any negotiation of the Palestinian issue, Prime Minister Begin preemptorily denounced the President's proposals. The Reagan Plan was, he said, a danger to the existence of the state of Israel and should be rejected as "a lifeless stillborn," and, to support his bristling negative, he extracted a 50-36 Knesset vote. In the course of the debate Begin shouted that Israel would keep unending control of the West Bank and Gaza. "We have no reason to get on our knees. No one will determine for us the borders of the Land of Israel."[56]

To show its contempt as well as defiance, the Begin government immediately announced a new, expanded settlements program. The Ministry of Defense would turn four military outposts in the West Bank into permanent civilian settlements, and forty-two new Israeli settlements would be established in the West Bank within the next four years. Over the next five years Israel would settle 100,000 additional Israelis in the West Bank, 20,000 in Golan, and 10,000 in Gaza. In addition, Israeli plans called for "a significant increase in settlements in Galilee and the Negev" that is, in Israel itself, where the number of Arab Israelis was increasing faster than that of Jewish Israelis.[57] The intentions of the Israeli hawks were perhaps most vividly expressed by General Ariel Sharon, who was reported as saying that Israel's invasion of Lebanon had rendered all talk of autonomy for West Bank Palestinians as irrelevant as were the post-1917 "White Russians in Paris cafés dreaming of the past."

President Reagan responded to this rejection of his proposals as though he were apologizing for his temerity in making them. Instead of using America's leverage to halt further settlements he augmented the annual subsidy paid to Israel by more than enough to pay the costs of accelerating the settlements program—and the Congress, not to be outdone, increased that tribute even further.

Comment:

President Reagan's September 1 speech was no doubt a well-intentioned initiative—although flawed by his explicit exclusion of the PLO and denial of self-determination for the Palestinians—but once more, as had happened so often with Israel, our government confused rhetoric with action, failing to recognize that words were meaningless without the will to make them effective. To call for negotiations without demonstrating that the United States was prepared to press the Israelis to freeze the settlements program foredoomed the effort to futility. The Israeli government had stated in a loud, clear and angry voice that it would not yield an inch of territory or give more than derisive meaning to autonomy. Since it had foreclosed all the important topics for discussion what incentives did the Arabs have to come and talk? No Arab nation could be expected to discuss a dictated peace while Israel was every day preempting more and more of the West Bank's land and water.

A more sensitive President might have been embarrassed by a thoughtless opinion he had earlier expressed. Prior administrations had consistently held that the settlements program was illegal under the Geneva Conventions and international law, but, soon after his election, Reagan had cavalierly remarked that the establishment of such settlements was "not necessarily improper." But, although that careless statement would have done no more than give Israel a debating point had he tried to persuade the Begin government to change its attitude, he seems to have dropped the issue altogether. Had he announced that America would stop subsidizing that "obstacle to peace" (the settlements are estimated to cost Israel roughly $200 million out of the $2.5 billion of our annual aid)[58] he could have brought the issue to a climax, but that would have been logical and, in the context of American-Israeli relations, logic is an orphan. Since, in the now stylized political vernacular, halting or reducing our annual subsidy would violate a sacrosanct injunction against "bringing pressure on Israel," the President accepted Jerusalem's scathing rejection without comment, making it clear to all the world, including King Hussein and the moderate Arab nations, that fruitful negotiations were impossible since the Israelis had ruled out any concessions and were continuing with increased speed to try to render the whole West Bank issue moot.

7

Israel Violates the Cease-Fire and Permits the Massacre

OUR MARINES WERE SENT TO LEBANON under the terms of a cease-fire arrangement that called for Israeli and Syrian, as well as PLO forces, to withdraw from West Beirut. Paragraph 2 of that agreement—to which Israel was a party—provided that it would be "scrupulously observed by all in Lebanon." The Reagan Administration announced that the Israeli goverment had given it assurances that it would keep its troops out of West Beirut as called for by the cease-fire.

In agreeing to leave Lebanon, Arafat's prime concern was for the safety of the Palesinian families left behind in the refugee camps. Since he and his colleagues were intensely aware of the danger of a bloodbath—particularly at the hands of the Maronite Phalange—he insisted on specific guarantees of their safety. Because Habib recognized that the concern of the PLO leaders was well founded, he demanded assurances from Begin as well as from Bashir Gemayel, the leader of the Phalange. Habib then staked the good name of the United States on the assurances he received.

The published plan of evacuation, subscribed to by all of the parties, contains the statement, in the section on "safeguards": "The Governments of Lebanon and the United States will provide appropriate guarantees of the safety . . . of law-abiding Palestinian noncombatants left in Beirut, including the families of those who have departed . . . The United States will provide its guarantees on the basis of assurances received from the government of Israel and from the leadership of certain groups with which it has been in contact." Habib also sent the following message to the Lebanese Prime Minister: "With reference to our many discussions . . . I am pleased to inform you that the Government of Israel has assured the United States Government that the plan for the departure of the PLO is acceptable. On the basis of these assurances, the United States Government is confident that the Government of Israel will not interfere with the implementation of this plan for the departure from Lebanon of the PLO leadership, officers, and combatants in a manner which will

"(A) assure the safety of such departing personnel;

"(B) assure the safety of other persons in the area . . .

"I would like to assure you that the United States Government fully

55

recognizes the importance of these assurances from the Government of Israel and that <u>my Government will do its utmost to insure that these assurances are scrupulously observed.</u>"[59] (underlining added)

The agreement negotiated by Philip Habib and accepted by Israel called for the evacuation from Beirut of 7,100 PLO combatants along with about 2,500 of their Syrian army and Syria-controlled Palestine Liberation Army allies. According to United States official count, about 8,300 PLO combatants left the country and 3,600 Syrian troops and PLA (Palestine Liberation Army) fighters also departed. Nevertheless on September 3, immediately following the completion of the evacuation on September 1, the IDF violated the cease-fire by moving troops into Moslem areas of West Beirut and into a residential section called Bir Hisan, north of the airport, claiming that there were still PLO supporters hiding there.[60]

All this was prelude to the tragedy that occurred following the assassination of Bashir Gemayel on September 14th. Within hours of that event, after clearance with Prime Minister Begin, the IDF flouted its commitments and pushed into West Beirut, taking control of the city. Responding as politics had conditioned him, President Reagan's first reaction was to excuse the IDF's move with the bland statement that "What led them [the Israeli forces] to move back in [sic] was the attack after the assassination of the elected President by some of the leftist militia that is still there in West Beirut."[61]

But by Thursday the President's more knowledgeable advisers had prevailed and the Administration expressed second thoughts. The entry of Israeli troops, it now asserted, was a "clear violation" of the cease-fire agreement and "contrary to assurances" given to the United States only two days before. There was, the White House and State Department announced in identical statements, "no justification in our view for Israel's continued military presence in West Beirut and we call for an immediate pullback." Meanwhile Arab opinion had concluded that America had encouraged, or at least approved the Israeli move, and Administration officials feared that, unless they took a firm stand and forced the withdrawal of Israeli forces, America's "credibility" would be severely damaged. Not for the first or last time was the Administation more alert to appearances than to the substance of the problem.

What followed was the usual ritual dance. Israel ignored the American *demarche* and Washington's voice became slightly, but only momentarily, shriller to the point where "several State Department officials" were quoted as saying—as though they hoped it were true but didn't believe it—that "a test of wills was now developing between the United States and Israel." For the first time since the invasion began the United States joined with other members of the United Nations Security Council in a unanimous condemnation of the Israeli advance, but only after it had tried unsuccessfully to get the word "condemnation" cut out of the final draft. The resolution gave Israel 24 hours to withdraw from West Beirut or at least to agree to do so.[62] But events were once again to show that, whenever the United States came eyeball-to-eyeball with Israel, it was our government that blinked.

By occupying West Beirut in violation of a commitment it had just given, the Israeli army took control of, and responsibility for, the Sabra and Shatila refugee camps. General Sharon and his colleagues then lost no time in opening the gates to their friend and ally, the Phalange, which set about butchering, as the Kahan Commission found, 700-800 Palestinian men, women and children* in an operation reminiscent of Tamerlane. Had the IDF high command merely wanted help in ferreting out PLO extremists in the camps, as they claimed, they could have done the job themselves or assigned the task to anti-Palestinian Shiite units of the Lebanese army, not the Phalange, whose reputation for compulsive massacre was notorious.[63]

Even after news of the massacre became widely known the Israeli government arrogantly refused to withdraw its forces from West Beirut. It was not until ten days after the massacre, when the world had been sickened by horror stories of the atrocity and even American Jewish organizations had begun to raise their voices, that the Israeli army began to withdraw.

In America our nation's responsibility for the whole tragic incident has gone largely unnoticed, yet the facts are clear enough. We put our own good faith behind Israel's word of honor; otherwise the PLO would never have agreed to leave. The PLO leaders trusted America's promise that Palestinians left behind would be safeguarded. When America promised to "do its utmost" to assure that Israel kept its commitments they took that commitment at face value. They would never have trusted an Israeli promise but they trusted us. We betrayed them.

Although the massacres revolted sensitive peoples throughout the world, no one seemed to blame the Reagan Administration for putting the United States in a position where it dishonored its word. The American press took almost no notice of the fact that, as a result of Israel's actions in violating the cease-fire and making possible the massacre, America had been put in a position of defaulting on its assurances to the PLO leaders as to the safety of the Palestinian families in the camps. But if our press showed an unbecoming reti-

---

* The Palestine Red Crescent put the number at over 2000, while death certificates were issued for 1200.

cence, the point was certainly not missed by the Arab nations. In a United Nations debate in the Security Council, the Jordanian representative declared that "Israel has chosen to lay bare the ability or the credibility" of the United States as the "guarantor of the Beirut agreement" and, as a consequence, added the representative of Kuwait, "there is no doubt that the American credibility is now at stake . . ."

In the end, the United States voted for a resolution condemning the "criminal massacre" but only after it had used its full political authority to rid the resolution of any mention of Israel. That did not, however, stop Israel's representative from denouncing the Security Council "for stooping to new depths of moral degeneration and depravity."

One can only imagine how differently Dwight Eisenhower would have reacted had the massacre occurred during his Presidency, with the word of the United States thus called into question. Not only would Israel have been formally held to account but he would have made clear his distaste for doing business with a government that continued to include General Sharon among its ministers.

If the American government showed no remorse for defaulting on its promise to the PLO leaders to "do its utmost" to assure that the Israeli government abided by the withdrawal arrangement, many Israelis felt shamed and sickened by the incident. Public support for the war, as shown by the polls, fell from 80% before the massacre to 45% in November and 34% in December.[64] The Israeli press was almost unanimous in its condemnation, many papers calling for the resignation of not merely Sharon and Begin, but the whole goverment. Nor was popular anger appeased when the government issued a statement: "No one will preach moral values or respect for human life to us. A blood libel has been perpetrated against the Jewish people." Such egregious insensitivity only increased the public protest until the demand for an inquiry became irresistible. Indeed, on Saturday night, one week after the massacres, as many as 400,000 — more than a tenth of Israel's Jewish population — demonstrated in Tel Aviv against what had occurred.

Finally even Begin was forced to agree to a judicial commission of inquiry, but, as with any such investigation, the so-called Kahan Commission did not please everyone. Many leaders of the Labor Party thought its finding of Israel's indirect responsibility was an understatement, while those sympathetic with Likud thought it far too harsh. Indeed, when the journalist Daniel Gavron visited Jerusalem's fruit market, a Likud stronghold, a day after the report was published, he discovered that not one of the 50-odd people with whom he talked liked the report; most thought the Commission had been too harsh and only one thought that Sharon should resign.[65]

By their public revulsion at the massacres the Israelis vindicated their reputation as a humane people. Yet the Begin Government disappointed many by its feeble response to the Kahan Report; it even continued Sharon as a member of the government, merely stripping him of the Defense Ministry. For all Menachem Begin's bluster, these events revealed him as an essentially weak leader.[66]

Just how the historians will view this period in Israel's history is hard to predict. Thoughtful Israelis were deeply disturbed by the revelation of sharp and passionate divisions of opinion within Israel's population—and their shock was increased immediately after the publication of the report when Peace Now activists were attacked by an ugly and angry mob and one activist was killed by a hurled grenade.

In retrospect it seems clear—and, in view of our government's past experience with Prime Minister Begin and his colleagues, it should have been clear at the time—that our country should never have pledged its official word in reliance on a Begin Government promise without an unequivocal determination to hold Israel to its commitments.

THE SECOND PHASE

(October 1982-May 1983)

AMERICA TRIES TO HELP ISRAEL ACHIEVE ITS SECOND
SET OF OBJECTIVES: A FRIENDLY LEBANON UNDER
ISRAELI INFLUENCE, A PEACE TREATY AND THE EXPUL-
SION FROM LEBANON OF THE SYRIAN ARMY.

8

We Again Commit Our Marines to a Peacekeeping Force

BECAUSE AMERICA'S CREDIBILITY HAD BEEN COMPROMISED by the Sabra and Shatila massacres, the Administration felt under special pressure to help contain the violence. Some outside presence was essential to prevent the whole area from bursting into flames.

Now, even more than at the time of the earlier deployment, the obvious—indeed the only sensible—solution was a United Nations force and such a force was readily available a few miles away on Lebanon's southern border with Israel. That force, known as UNIFIL and consisting of 5,300 men, had been stationed there since March 1978 and it now had nothing to do. Some UNIFIL contingents could have been promptly moved into Beirut from the south and the depleted units later replaced. There is no doubt that the White House would have liked to pass the responsibility to the United Nations, and Congressional sentiment insisted that a UNIFIL redeployment be explored.

Under these circumstances why did the Administration not seize on the UNIFIL solution? When Israel and the United States hold opposing views the outcome is preordained, so once again the Israelis had their way. In spite of American urging Israel made clear that it would not permit the UNIFIL units to move north through the IDF's lines. "We certainly hope Israel will agree to a UNIFIL move," Anita Stockman, a State Department spokesman, announced plaintively. But, of course, it did not, and, once again, by conditioned reflex, our government gave in without even a whimper.[67] After all, as Prime Minister Begin had made clear, since President Reagan was not God he could be safely ignored. So, contrary to justice and precedent, the aggressor nation for the second time fixed the terms for sweeping up the chaos it had left in its wake.

Israel is said to have opposed a United Nations force on the ground that some of its component units might come from countries unfriendly to it, but that could hardly be said of the countries providing the UNIFIL force—France, Finland, Fiji, Ireland, Ghana, Italy, the Netherlands, Norway, Senegal and Sweden. Still Israel had reason to dislike UNIFIL; it had committed what, to the Israelis, was *lèse-majesté* in June 1982, when, unable to offer effective armed resistance, UNIFIL units had found a variety of means, consistent with their mandate, to impede the IDF in its rampage toward Beirut.[68]

In addition to Israel's detestation of the United Nations it may have had an even more potent reason for obstructionism; it could well have calculated that, by engaging our country more deeply in Lebanon, it could assure our continued help in achieving its objectives. After all, Israel's leaders knew—and often boasted—that they could control America's actions.

So once more we deployed our marines to Beirut. If the duration of the first commitment had been too brief, the duration of the proposed new deployment of our forces was, in the nature of things, indeterminant and therefore too long. On the first occasion the objective of the marines' mission had defined the time span of their tour, since they were to stay only until the departure of the PLO. But their new mission was expressed in far more general terms; they would remain until "all foreign forces were withdrawn"—yet neither the Israelis nor the Syrians were showing any intention of leaving. As a result our marine contingent had become a military force with no coherent mission, and, in tactical terms, a force without a mission has no *raison d'être* for deployment.

Since no one seemed to know just what the marines were supposed to do nor was any clarification made later, the terms of their projected stay was left in great confusion with the Administration shifting carelessly from one formulation to another. Nicholas A. Veliotes, Assistant Secretary of State for Near Eastern and South Asian Affairs, in testifying on September 29, 1982, before the House Foreign Affairs Committee, offered a "clarification" which stated that Israeli-Syrian withdrawal was not a "criterion", only an "expectation", and that the troops would be gone by the end of 1982 as an "outer limit."[69]

Comment:

Once again Israel had pushed us into a role we should never have undertaken. One error had built on another. If we had treated Israel as we treated other nations and held it to its commitments, it would not have dared to break the cease-fire agreement so cavalierly. Had we stood firm when Israel rejected a United Nations peacekeeping force, America could have avoided the death of almost three hundred marines. By failing to insist on our nation's rights and protect its interests, the Administration permitted Israel to maneuver us into a costly and dangerous quagmire.

9

The Secretary of State Tries to Mediate the Negotiation of a Lebanese-Israeli Peace Agreement

AN ESSENTIAL PART OF ISRAEL'S GRAND DESIGN in launching its invasion had been to force the Lebanese government to grant it a full peace treaty that would, among other things, assure Israel control of South Lebanon—through, among other instruments, its hired mercenary, Major Sa'ad Haddad and his private army. But events did not work out as planned. Almost from the beginning of the invasion Bashir Gemayel had disappointed Israeli leaders; his Phalange failed to provide more than half-hearted help to the IDF in its military operations and Lebanon's president-elect further disenchanted Begin and Sharon when they summoned him to a meeting at a government guest house in northern Israel on September 1 and presented a list of their demands.

That meeting got off to a rough start; indeed Begin seems to have intended that it should, since he deliberately kept Bashir Gemayel waiting for two hours. Begin abruptly rejected Bashir's explanation as to why he could not sign the kind of peace treaty Israel wanted, and Begin and Sharon expressed scorn and derision at Bashir's substitute offer of a non-aggression pact. Further disagreement arose regarding the role of Major Haddad, the head of Israel's private army in south Lebanon, whom Begin had brought with him to the meeting. In spite of the fact that Bashir had planned to put Haddad on trial for dereliction of duty and treasonable trafficking with Israel, Begin now demanded that Haddad be appointed as the new government's Defense Minister or at least as its army commander. When Bashir emphatically ruled that out, Begin, it is reported, assumed his most arrogant, hectoring tone, implying that Israel was now top dog and Bashir had better go along if he knew what was good for him. At the end, the meeting deteriorated into a shouting match.[70]

Bashir Gemayel was expressing far more than his own views in rejecting the outrageous Israeli demands. He knew that Begin's ultimatum would be clearly unacceptable to the Moslem Lebanese and even to more moderate Phalangists; they were not prepared to be liberated from the Palestinians and Syrians only to submit to dictation by Israel. By the time of Bashir's violent death just a fortnight later, he had

63

already made clear that he would not play the sedulous ape to Israel's autocratic leader; he well knew the ferocity of Lebanese politics and he did not dare turn his back on his country's factional politics or appear too complicitous with Israel. As a result, since Lebanon is always ripe soil for devil theories, many Moslem leaders inevitably attributed his assassination to the Israelis, while Israel blamed the Syrians, and Bashir's supporters blamed the former Lebanese President, Suleiman Franjieh. Franjieh had a valid reason for disliking Bashir since a few years previously the Phalange had murdered his son and thirty other family members and supporters.

If the Israelis were disappointed with Bashir it was because they had entertained excessive expectations. Of all the Maronite leaders, Bashir had clearly been Israel's closest friend. He had made the initial approaches to secure help from Israel and the Israelis had played a significant role in making him President. Their commanding military presence in the area where the polling took place could not help but influence some members of the Parliament and Israel had actively assisted Bashir to pick up the 5 to 10 final votes necessary to secure the two-thirds majority of the Parliament required for election. That majority had not been easy to achieve because the Moslem leaders of West Beirut, the parliamentary representatives from Tripoli and the Northern Bekaa Valley, and even a few Maronite delegates had chosen to boycott the election. So the Israeli Defense Ministry had produced a team of experts who, among other things, worked hard to secure the support of the faction led by Camille Chamoun, the opposition candidate, and even provided a helicopter to collect one elderly delegate.

But if the Israelis had expected too much from Bashir, they were darkly suspicious of his brother Amin. From the beginning Amin had served as the family's liaison with Damascus and he favored closer relations with Syria rather than Israel. He had been largely frozen out by Bashir as an effective voice among the Maronites and had been plainly angered when his brother won the presidency.[71] Thus, rather than embracing Amin as Bashir's successor, the Israelis toyed briefly with a scheme to avoid a new presidential election and have Elias Sarkis, the outgoing President, appoint a military government headed by Sarkis' old crony, Colonel Jonny Abdu. At this point, however, the American government had thrown its influence on the side of Amin, which was a critical mistake since Abdu was not only very friendly to America but had a much broader political base and was far more acceptable to the Shiites and other Islamic elements. In any event the Americans had their way, and, on September 21, the Lebanese Parliament elected Amin Gemayel president by a majority of 77 votes, including many Moslem delegates who had boycotted Bashir's election but were prepared to support Amin because they saw him as a candidate of the United States rather than Israel.[72]

Still, in spite of the fact that all had not worked out as expected, the Israelis were far from ready to abandon their long-held plan for a full peace treaty. The United States was their ever-indulgent friend, and they hoped that by inducing America to lean hard enough on President Amin Gemayel, his government might still be persuaded to conclude the kind of document they wanted. After all, the American government's proclaimed objective was to secure the withdrawal of all foreign forces from Lebanon, and Israel was conditioning its withdrawal on a full-fledged peace treaty.

Unhappily the negotiation for such a treaty proved long and querulous. Gemayel was under pressure from Moslem elements not to grant Israel the special rights it demanded in southern Lebanon; such a concession, they contended, would amount to a humiliating disguised annexation by Israel of the south, which was largely inhabited by Shiites. So Israel pursued the tactic of prolonging the haggling over such frivolous questions as the venue of the negotiations and the level of the negotiators, while America increased pressure on both Lebanese and Israelis. In time, however, that reached a point of diminishing returns. The Israeli public was growing increasingly unhappy over the disturbing rate of casualties suffered by the IDF and the Israelis lost faith in the negotiations Secretary of State Shultz was now actively directing.

Despite its doubtful wisdom as a diplomatic move, Shultz's direct intervention was understandable in personal terms. Only recently appointed Secretary of State, he obviously wished to prove his competence, while the Administration yearned for some diplomatic *tour de force* to relieve its consistently bleak record of failure. So Shultz committed America's authority and prestige to try to bludgeon the Gemayel government into granting Israel as much control over southern Lebanon as it could be persuaded to concede.

Except for the Americans directly involved, no one was happy with the agreement finally reached on May 17, even though major concessions to Israel were included in secret protocols, with the published text containing only those understandings least offensive to Moslem public opinion. Still, to most Lebanese (including many Maronites) and to the Syrians, it represented an excessive derogation of sovereignty and they were also offended by the "normalization of relations" promise it contained; to the Israelis it offered far less control of southern Lebanon than they had hoped to achieve, while lacking the character of a full peace treaty. So the Israeli government revised its tactics. As Prime Minister Begin implied to his close supporters on the home front, he was engaging in a charade. His government had signed the agreement, he indicated, only to gain favor with the Americans and repair slightly strained relations with Washington. To assure Israel concessions that would, if known, be anathema to Moslem Lebanese— he had demanded and obtained a number of secret protocols, including a secret side letter from the American negotiators saying that the IDF would not have to withdraw from Lebanon unless the Syrians agreed to withdraw at the same time. Since Begin could foresee that, once the agreement was signed, the Syrians would refuse to withdraw, he was confident that Israel would not have to abide by the agreement.[73]

Meanwhile, to satisfy the rituals of domestic politics, the charade went forward in the Knesset. The Begin Government tried to pass off the agreement as equivalent to the coveted peace treaty that justified the war; the Labor opposition denounced it as no better than the original armistice agreement worked out in 1949. Certainly it did not satisfy the hopes of most Israelis, who wished more than anything else for the immediate return of their sons and husbands serving in the IDF and to be rid of the whole Lebanese headache.

But, if the agreement made Israelis unhappy, it left Amin Gemayel in the worst possible position, with his position in Lebanon critically undermined. Because of Secretary Shultz's highly visible intervention, Amin was inevitably accused of caving in to the United States, while disgruntled factions in Lebanon expressed outrage at the degree of his concessions to Israel. Caught between these forces, Amin tried desperately to temporize, evading formal ratification to placate the Moslems, while implying an intention to ratify to please the right-wing Maronites.

Not only was the agreement flawed by its qualification of Lebanon's sovereignty, but Shultz's diplomatic insensitivity destroyed any chance of its acceptance. Although, in taking personal charge of the negotiation, the Secretary may have at least subconsciously sought to emulate Henry Kissinger's success in the Second Sinai negotiations, he lacked the experience for such an endeavor. In 1974 Kissinger had been sharply aware of the need to gauge precisely what President Assad needed before he accepted a deal between Israel and Egypt so he had kept constantly in touch with the Syrian Government. But Shultz blandly ignored Syria's pride and its political and security requirements. Apparently relying on ambiguous assurances from moderate Arab countries and—so the rumor goes—disregarding the advice of the American embassy in Damascus, he turned his back on the Syrians, while expressing confidence that Syria would withdraw once Israel had agreed to do so.[74]

When Secretary Shultz visited Damascus on May 7 the Syrians were apparently expecting that he would discuss with them such modifications of the agreement with Israel as they might require; instead he simply outlined the terms that had been agreed with the Israelis, presenting them as a *fait accompli* and suggesting no modifications whatever to satisfy Syrian needs.[75] It even seemed that the Administration wished to discourage any serious discussions with President Assad, since six days later on May 13, Secretary of Defense Weinberger threatened "retaliatory force" against Syria. So it was hardly surprising that, when our government sent Ambassador Habib to Damascus on May 18, Syrian officials indignantly refused to receive him.

In repeatedly assuring the world that Syria would withdraw its troops if a Lebanese-Israeli agreement was reached, both the State Department and the White House either misunderstood or deliberately misstated Syria's position. Spokesmen for Syria, including President Assad, had made it clear that its troops would leave Lebanon only *after* Israeli forces had withdrawn and then only if the Lebanese government's authority extended to the Israeli border. But that condition was far from satisfied by the May 17 agreement; Israel had rejected an unconditional withdrawal, insisting instead on rights and privileges that seriously qualified Lebanese sovereignty.

The Reagan Administration seemed never able to define a clear position. At the time of the invasion on June 6, 1982, our government had voted for a United Nations Security Council resolution which had been unanimously approved. That resolution called for Israel's complete departure from Lebanese territory. In supporting the conditions Israel was now demanding as the price of withdrawal President Reagan was not only reversing his Administration's earlier position, he was also rejecting the principle President Eisenhower had announced and supported when he forced the Israelis to withdraw from the Sinai following the Suez affair in 1956: 'Should a nation which attacks and occupies foreign territory in the face of United Nations disapproval be allowed to impose conditions on its own withdrawal? The United Nations must not fail."

In the face of mounting evidence to the contrary, Secretary Shultz and President Reagan continued to issue upbeat bulletins. At a news conference on May 17, the day the agreement was signed, the President observed that he was confident Syria would now withdraw its troops "because of pressure from other Arab countries." That declaration presumably reflected the original qualified statements of support coming from Saudi Arabia, Jordan, Egypt and Algeria. But as the secret agreements became known and it was realized what the Gemayel government was seeking to downplay—the fact that the agreement provided not only for special Israeli rights in southern Lebanon but the "termination of the state of war between" Israel and Lebanon—that support melted away.

Israel's strategem of accepting an unacceptable document, then assuring its failure by conditioning its own withdrawal on the simultaneous withdrawal by the Syrians, was a well-conceived ploy. As Begin had foreseen, his government received high credit from President Reagan for its statesmanship in agreeing to a highly qualified withdrawal (that was, in reality, no withdrawal at all). At the same time, Israel's agreement deflected the President's wrath toward Syria for upholding Lebanese territorial integrity. At a press conference, after Syria had once more made its position clear with regard to the May 17 agreement, President Reagan displayed his habitual poetic license when dealing with unpleasant facts by observing that Assad had "reneged." It can be argued, on the contrary, that Assad was the only party who has pursued a consistent course, while America neglected its duty to protect Lebanese sovereignty from its powerful southern neighbor.

Comment:

How any American government could have so wildly misread the reactions of Damascus will no doubt puzzle future historians. As the Syrians see it, their army had not invaded Lebanon as the IDF had done; it had gone there in 1976 under a mandate from the Arab league and on the invitation of the Lebanese government to help save that government from the PLO and other Moslem elements, and—like the man who came to dinner—it had stayed on under that invitation for more than six years. Moreover, because the whole of Lebanon had been a part of Syria for 14 years between 1918 and 1932 until the French carved out the new—and in many ways—artificial entity of Lebanon, the Syrians still thought of Lebanon as a part of what, in an Israeli phrase, might be called Eretz Syria.

But Syria's interest in Lebanon did not derive solely from history. If Israel felt security concerns with regard to southern Lebanon, Syria had legitimate security reasons for maintaining its forces in the Beka'a Valley. It had shown that concern in the summer of 1981, when the Phalangists had widened and paved a dirt road to connect their heartland on the western side of the mountains with Zahle, the provincial capital of the Valley. The Syrians had responded by forcing them out of the town. Although that action did not involve or threaten Israel, Begin, with a great show of toughness and sanctimony (presumably for domestic consumption since he was facing elections in June) announced melodramatically that he would not allow the Christians to be annihilated in Lebanon and on April 18 had sent the IDF to shoot down two Syrian troop-carrying helicopters. In response Syria had moved three batteries of SAM-6s (surface-to-air missiles) into the Valley. It had taken combined Saudi and American diplomacy to defuse the crisis.

Against this background it was naive to assume that the Syrians would withdraw from the Beka'a Valley (where Israel had attacked their forces only ten months before) so long as Israel maintained patrols to operate in territory adjoining the Syrian frontier under the terms of the May 17 agreement. Syria had already felt its security threatened when Israel conquered, and later annexed, the strategic Golan Heights; with guns and rockets mounted on that high ground, Israel could bombard Syria's capital, Damascus, at any time. In addition, Israel had acquired a new surveillance base on the Barouk Mountain high over the Beka'a Valley from which its radar could penetrate into central Syria, thus providing it with battlefield surveillance in a future war. Israeli planes could, and had, flown up the Beka'a before turning East to attack Damascus, while ground attacks through the Valley could be directed at the Syrian city of Homs, the headquarters of Syrian communications. All this gave reality to a Syrian nightmare of a pincer movement that would involve the Lebanese Phalange attacking from the northeast and Israel attacking from the south—which was precisely the strategy that the Israelis had contemplatedwhile conniving with Bashir Gemayel.[76]

A less obtuse American diplomacy would have recognized Syria's security concerns and predicted that, if Israel were offered a security zone, the Syrians would inevitably insist on a comparable zone of their own. Thus, America might, by collaborating with all three parties— Syria, Lebanon and Israel—have tried to arrange an overall settlement responsive not merely to Israeli, but also Syrian requirements. To be sure, such an agreement might have seriously compromised the authority of the Gemayel government, but it would have had the support of Syria and thus might have been made acceptable to the Islamic elements in Lebanon—support that would never be forthcoming for an agreement according a privileged position only for Israel. But instead of recognizing that it had blundered into a *cul de sac* and urgently needed to revise its tactics, the Administration continued to put pressure on Amin Gemayel to reject any modification of the May 17 agreement. Indeed it continued that pressure long after it was clear that the existence of the agreement disabled Gemayel from broadening the base of his government in order to survive as president. In the end, as might have been predicted, Gemayel was forced by opposition elements in Lebanon to renounce the agreement—an action which, under the circumstances, was interpreted as a defeat for America and a victory for Syria.

Blind to the nuances of a complex situation, the Administration continued to condemn Syria's "refusal" to withdraw as the "principal obstacle to peace in Lebanon". That accusation quite overlooked the fact that Syria was on record as consistently offering to pull its troops out of Lebanon as a part of a complete and unqualified withdrawal of all foreign forces—Israeli, Syrian and the PLO.

Why did the Administration take such an insensitive position and hold it to the point of inevitable defeat? Some who try to explain all seemingly irrational actions in terms of human frailities have suggested that Secretary Shultz acted out of personal pique at Assad's cool reception to what he had regarded as his personal diplomatic triumph. That motive, they suggest, explains the Administration's abrupt decision to offer Israel a "Strategic Cooperation Agreement"—commonly referred to as an "alliance"—which will be discussed later.

THE THIRD PHASE

(June 1983-February 1984)

FAILING TO ACHIEVE THE PEACE TREATY IT WANTED
AND FINDING THE GEMAYEL GOVERNMENT TOO WEAK
AN INSTRUMENT TO SERVE ITS OBJECTIVES, ISRAEL
ABANDONS ITS GRAND DESIGN, WITHDRAWING THE
IDF TO SOUTHERN LEBANON AND THUS LEAVING OUR
MARINES EXPOSED TO FIRE. ALTHOUGH THIS DESTROYS
ANY CHANCE TO ACHIEVE A UNITED LEBANON FREE
FROM FOREIGN TROOPS, THE ADMINISTRATION STILL
PERSISTS IN PURSUING THAT WILL-O'-THE-WISP.

10

Israel Moves the IDF South out of Danger

BY THE MIDDLE OF 1983 IT BECAME CLEAR to the government in Jerusalem (though not to Washington) that Israel's long-planned Lebanese design was dead as a haddock. The Israelis had learned from disillusioning experience that an Israeli-dominated Maronite government in Beirut would be so compromised that it could not extend its writ throughout the country; such a combination of strength and accommodation was an unresolvable contradiction. Their next best course, as they saw it, was to continue to occupy southern Lebanon and thus secure by force what they could not achieve by treaty. Trying by military means to prop up a weak Gemayel regime was proving too costly both in financial and political terms and in the lives of its soldiers. The IDF was taking casualties, particularly in the Chouf Mountains, and the Israeli public was demanding the return of the troops. The new Defense Minister Moshe Arens, who had had no responsibility for launching the invasion, clearly wanted to redeploy to the south where his troops would be less vulnerable.[77]

The Begin government seemed quite unconcerned that the abandonment of its grand design might embarrass the Reagan Administration which had now become an overt supporter of the Gemayel Government. If America were foolish enough to pursue an objective Israel had discarded as unfeasible, that was Washington's decision; the Israelis would not smooth our path by agreeing to the abrogation of the May 17 agreement even though it was now clear that that document would never become effective.

Israel's move was in the time-honored spirit of *sauve qui peut* and, heeding the message, a prudent American government would have devised means to clear out also. But, having trapped itself by its overly exuberant rhetoric, the Administration did not have the faintest idea what to do. It had fallen victim to the same mistake America had made in Vietnam—the belief that, with resolute will and vast resources, America could mix in the internal affairs of a small country with exotic customs and values and effectively impose a *papier mâché* regime on all the warring factions. So, in spite of the danger flags noisily flapping, the President held steady on course, faithfully validating George Santyana's definition of a fanatic as one who redoubles his efforts when he has

72

forgotten his aim. He seemed obsessed with the thought that we could frighten the Syrians into withdrawing from Lebanon by a mighty show of military muscle—which, someone should have told him, was a cruel exercise in futility against as sturdy an antagonist as President Assad.

Our Marines In the Cross-Fire

Not only did the Israeli withdrawal leave America without a partner in Israel's grand Lebanese design but the departure of the IDF from the Chouf Mountains put our Marines in jeopardy. The IDF had occupied those mountains early in its Lebanon invasion but that occupation had not been a congenial exercise. The Druse together with Shiites and Christians had made their homes in that high ground for centuries, and they had become famous for the ferocity with which they had again and again defended their homeland. When the Maronite Christians tried to seize control of the area in 1860, the Druse had massacred them; then, during the civil war in the 1970s, the Druse had again repulsed Maronite invaders. The hatred between the Druse and the Phalange had such a long and intense history that the winner in any conflict could be expected to make corpses of the losing side.

During their long connivance with the Phalange, the Israelis had also intrigued with the Druse. Practicing the crude power politics of arming both sides and playing one off against the other, they had sought to prevent either faction from attaining too much power. At the same time, they had tried to avoid appearing in opposition to Druse interests in deference to the substantial Druse population in Israel (represented by a seat in the Knesset) which they did not wish to offend.

As has often happened, the Israelis overplayed their hand. While occupying the Chouf Mountains, they invited their co-conspirators, the Phalange, to enter Druse villages, parade up and down and subject the residents to insults. During July 1982, in the village of Suq al Gharb, the IDF's admission of a Phalange battalion resulted in clashes with the Druse that left a number of dead and wounded. In the village of Bayt al-Din the entry of a Phalange company produced bloody acts of revenge.[78] Thus, once the IDF withdrew without ensuring the withdrawal of the Phalange, a fierce fight was inevitable.

In anticipation of that event the Druse leader, Walid Jumblatt, prudently sought to safeguard his people from a massacre, such as the Phalange had perpetrated in the Sabra and Shatila camps. Through Druse friends in Syria, he obtained arms and equipment to prepare his forces for the inevitable battle when the Israelis withdrew, and he did not have long to wait.[79] Nor did our marines. Based next door to a Lebanese Army unit at the Beirut airport just beneath the overhanging mountains; they would—once the IDF withdrew—be inevitably exposed to cross-fire between the Lebanese Army with help of the Phalange and Druse forces defending their homeland area. That was obvious.

But, although the IDF commanders well understood what was in store, they shrugged their shoulders; if the Americans chose to leave their marines in the line of fire, that was their problem and it would not affect Israel's withdrawal plans. The only concession they made to our American negotiator, Robert McFarlane, was to delay redeployment until August 31, to permit the Lebanese Army and Moslem militias to battle it out in West Beirut.[80]

As was predictable, our marines began taking their first casualties in June, 1983, only days after Israel announced its plans to withdraw and amid mounting opposition to the May 17 agreement. On August 29 two marines were killed and 14 others wounded and, on September 6, rocket fire killed two more and wounded three others. Meanwhile, the Druse and Shiites fought the Phalange and the Lebanese Army so effectively that, after a few weeks, they controlled all coast roads south of the airport and almost all of the Chouf Mountains, while our marines suffered the usual fate of innocent bystanders. They were not the targets of the rockets or shells that hit them; they were simply in the line of fire between the warring factions. On September 18, General Paul X. Kelley, Commandant of the Marine Corps, said, "Whoever is shooting at us . . . is shooting more at where we are than who we are. There is no indication anybody is purposefully taking marines under fire." And when, on September 26, 1983, a cease-fire was declared, Deputy Assistant Secretary of State Robert H. Pelletreau told a Congressional Committee: "We believe there is no concerted effort to target the marines. But they're in an area where there is violence."[81]

Comment:

When it was clear that Israel had abandoned hope that the Maronite government it had installed could achieve control over a Lebanon free of Syrian forces, our government should have recognized the implications and promptly withdrawn our marines. But, even though it was obvious that the IDF's evacuation of the Chouf would greatly heighten the risk to our embattled forces, we took no effective action to deter Israel from pulling out. That raises at least two questions the Administration has not adequately answered:

1. Why, since it was evident that the IDF's evacuation of the Chouf would expose our marines to cross-fire, did we accept Israel's decision with only mild remonstrances, yet continue to deploy our marines at the airport?

2. Why, when Israel, by withdrawing its troops, clearly recognized that the Gemayel government could not gain control of Lebanon so long as the May 17 agreement remained extant, did the Administration still strongly oppose the abrogation of that agreement while continuing to admonish the Gemayel government to broaden its political base? Wasn't it clear that those two positions were mutually contradictory?

11

The U.S. Becomes Directly Involved

ONCE THE ISRAELIS HAD ANNOUNCED that they were withdrawing, the Administration should have acted promptly to save our marines from death and injury. It should have invoked the old legal doctrine of *rebus sic stantibus* (circumstances alter cases) and explained to the Lebanese Government and other interested parties that several developments, including the Israeli withdrawal, had materially altered the conditions under which the marines had been originally deployed; thus they could no longer perform their assigned mission. Peacekeeping forces were never intended to remain exposed to violence; the United Nations had provided ample precedent for withdrawing peacekeeping forces when cease-fires broke down and those forces could no longer fulfill their mission.[82] So the Administration would not have appeared cowardly or irresponsible had it, in consultation with the other members of the multinational force, developed a schedule for prompt withdrawal.

But, instead of concentrating on trying to extricate our troops from an untenable situation, the Administration committed them to active participation in the fighting. Our Government not only authorized the marines to fire at the Druse who were defending themselves from the Maronites, but it also began to use the powerful guns of the huge fleet we had deployed offshore. Since we were, the President now said, assisting the Lebanese army to capture the Druse mountain positions, our fleet continued to fire its guns and use its planes to bomb the Druse, even when the marine commander publicly stated that our troops were not at the moment in danger.[83]

Such a drastic rewriting of our marines' mission should have evoked vigorous resistance on the home front, but at this point even the War Powers Act was scarcely mentioned. What blunted any effort to confront the issue was that no one in Washington knew what the marines were supposed to be achieving. Although the newspapers still referred to them as "peacekeepers" there was no peace to be kept, and the President's careless comments only compounded the confusion. On September 20, 1982, he announced our marines would have "the mission of enabling the Lebanese government to resume full sovereignty over its capital—the essential pre-condition for extending its control over the entire country"—a role that had nothing to do with peacekeeping, as that phrase has historically been used. The classical function of a peacekeeping force is to separate warring factions, not to help one faction prevail over another. But from the beginning the White House got the issue all mixed up.

Only a few hours after the marines arrived, the President had announced that they would leave Beirut only when assured by the Lebanese authorities that the Lebanese government could itself provide for the nation's security. On October 24, 1983, the President faithfully echoed the rhetoric of Vietnam days by telling reporters that the United States had "vital interests" in Lebanon because "if Lebanon ends up under the tyranny of forces hostile to the West, not only will our strategic position in the Eastern Mediterranean be threatened, but also the stability of the entire Middle East." Still, he made clear that the threat of such an horrific loss did not justify beefing up our forces. On November 14,1983, he commented that if there were a "collapse of order" in Lebanon, that would be a reason for the marines to leave. Then, trying to clarify that obscure statement a week later, he said that if a new government should emerge in Lebanon and began moving "in a different direction . . . then I suppose that would be a reason for bringing them out."[84]

The smog darkened even more as the Pentagon, which had originally advised reporters that the marines would not engage in "combat" but would be withdrawn if major fighting broke out, kept the marines at their posts in the midst of major fighting. When they began suffering the casualties from cross-fire that were inevitable once the Israelis departed, the Administration behaved as though the Druse were America's enemy. To reconcile fantasy with doctrine, Administration spokesmen and many of our press and television commentators now began referring to the Druse and indeed any others opposed to the Gemayel regime—a majority of the Lebanese in fact—as "leftist forces". Our national dialogue became a muddle of tags and slogans disguised as concepts. As one Congressman put it during a television appearance I witnessed, we were fighting for our "ally", the Gemayel government.

Our creeping—or more accurately, our fumbling, stumbling—involvement followed an insidious course.

At first United States warships were authorized to fire at Druse and Shiite artillery positions to protect our marines; later they were no longer restricted to returning fire but were authorized to use artillery and air strikes to support the Lebanese army. After that, United States aircraft commenced provocative overflights of Syrian artillery positions in Syrian-controlled territory.

When that bombing resulted in an American casualty (and the capture of the now-famous Lieutenant Goodman) we reverted to naval shelling, even though that was far less precise and far more likely to produce civilian casualties.

Finally our navy began bombarding Druse positions near the town of Suq al Gharb in direct support of Lebanese army units, while several of our marine officers were seen in Suq al Gharb during the middle of the battle "gathering information" to help our warships coordinate targets.[85]

Thus, step by step, America permitted itself to be drawn more deeply into direct participation in the Lebanese civil war in pursuit of an objective the Israelis had already abandoned. No longer were we a peacekeeper even by the President's elastic jargon.[86] Without offering an intelligible public explanation he had assigned our forces the totally different mission of helping the Lebanese Government try to extend its writ by force (and with it the writ of the Phalange) to the whole of Lebanon— although events had plainly shown such an objective to be quite unattainable.

Comment:

That abrupt transformation of the marines' role displayed not only shockingly bad judgment but a disturbing ignorance of history. In engaging our marines and the guns of our fleet to help Gemayel conquer the dissident factions in his country, we were repeating with almost eerie fidelity our failed adventure in Vietnam. Just as earlier Presidents had done in South East Asia, President Reagan was once again committing American forces—and American prestige—to try to help a weak, narrowly-based government, supported by only a narrow faction, impose control on highly motivated rival factions which, as with the North Vietnamese, were being armed by a neighboring country. As in Vietnam we were operating in an unfamiliar environment in a tortured area far from America that was really not a nation and in which we had only a limited interest. In Vietnam we had failed to achieve our goal even after committing 560,000 men; in Lebanon we sought to accomplish an impossible objective with only 1800 marines, supported by U.S. naval ships firing guns from offshore.

There is much reason to believe that the President's attitude toward the complex problems of Lebanon was strongly influenced by his conviction that all problems can be traced to the Soviet Union—or at least to what he calls "Marxist-Leninism." Inspired by that conviction he employed a convoluted logic to produce a curious syllogism. The fact that the Druse obtained arms from Syrians made them, *ipso facto*, surrogates of the Syrians. Since the Syrians in turn obtained arms from Moscow, they thus became instruments of the Kremlin. It therefore followed, Q.E.D., that a successful Druze repulse of the Maronite invaders would be a triumph for a Soviet Union that was "seeking to take over the Middle East"—and ultimately, of course, the world.

Such, apparently, was how our Lebanese predicament appeared through the White House window, or, in other words, as seen through a glass darkly. The complex elements that had long made Lebanon a cockpit of feuding factions were omitted from the President's oversimplified equation. No doubt his Manichean view provided useful salve to our national conscience; if the fighting in Lebanon were part of America's long-running contest with the "evil empire", we were justified in joining in the killing. Who cared about the facts? Without that geopolitical gloss the Lebanese civil war would have lacked much television value; it would have been relegated to off-hour viewing as merely another local conflict that only lightly touched our interests.

12

The Marine Slaughter

THE ADMINISTRATION'S FOLLY in committing American Marines to the hate-filled environment of Lebanon was tragically demonstrated on October 23, 1983 when a truck bomb destroyed the marine headquarters at the Beirut airport and killed 265 Americans. Almost simultaneously another truck bomb hit the French unit of the peace-keeping force and killed 59. On November 4 a similar operation at Israeli headquarters killed 60.[87]

The intelligence communities in all three countries agreed that the terrorist acts had been committed by an extremist fanatic group of Iranian-backed Shiites (who call themselves "Islamic Jihad") living near Baalbek in eastern Lebanon. But, searching compulsively for a more lurid conspiracy theory, the President announced that he was "more determined than ever" that the perpetrators "cannot take over that vital and strategic area of the earth."[88] It was an instinctive but irrational reaction. He could go no farther in associating the alleged authors of the crime with the Kremlin since the Iranian Shias detested the Soviets quite as fiercely as he did. But there were always the Syrians. The terrorists could not, Administration spokesmen suggested, have carried out their lethal mission without Syrian complicity.

Following their habitual pattern, the Israelis responded to the attack on their forces by bombing a purported Shiite terrorist headquarters near Baalbek on November 14. The French bombed it again on November 17. There was, it was rumored, considerable sentiment in Washington for the United States to follow with a final raid that would complete the demolition of the same target—a proposal quite possibly devised by someone who had read Agatha Christie's *Murder on the Orient Express*, where the avengers take turn thrusting a dagger into the same victim in order to collectivize the guilt. But largely, so it was rumored, at the urging of the Secretary of Defense and the Joint Chiefs of Staff, the United States held back.

Comment:

This time the Administration did not imitate the Israelis in an action that would have been out of character for America. Having let our country become entangled in Lebanon's internal feuds, we would have made our position far worse by engaging in the kind of two eyes-for-a-tooth practice that Israel has regularly pursued—responding to any terrorist action by ritually smashing up Arab villages and killing many more civilians than terrorists. No great power that prides itself on justice and humanity could engage in such a practice without compromising the integrity of its principles. [89]

13

The Administration Ties America More Tightly to Israel

IN ASSERTING HIS DOGMATIC FAITH in the universal culpability of the Communist conspiracy, which required that Syria be regarded as a Soviet instrument because it accepted some Russian military aid, the President was implicitly ignoring America's own experience. Just because the United States equips Israel's armed forces with highly advanced weapons and equipment, would anyone seriously argue that Israel is merely an American stooge? Is not the reverse more accurate? No one acquainted with the Syrian scene would regard President Assad as anything but his own man; Henry Kissinger merely confirmed the experience of others when in 1974 he found him "a supreme nationalist."[90] Not only is he fiercely independent but he has deliberately flaunted his independence of Moscow, as, for example, when he rejected Soviet admonitions on behalf of Arafat.

He is, moreover, a strong and determined leader and the Administration showed a lamentable naivete when it undertook to frighten him into withdrawing his forces from Lebanon. Instead of caving in to American pressures, the Syrians responded by stepping up their military assistance to the Lebanese factions opposed to the Gemayel government. Washington's instinctive *riposte* was to increase military pressure, with unconscionable disregard of civilian casualties, by bombarding Druse and Shiite positions with the New Jersey's 16-inch guns—which at that distance are not only inaccurate but fantastically destructive.

Had we learned anything from our dolorous experience during preceding years, we should clearly have recognized the costs and dangers of uncritically supporting every Israeli adventure, automatically forgiving every Israeli broken promise, obediently sweeping up the breakage left by Israel's destructive actions, doggedly pursuing Israel's imperialistic Lebanese design even after the Israelis had themselves abandoned it as hopeless, and turning the other cheek at the rudeness and disdain shown America by Israel's leaders. Once the PLO had been evacuated the Administration should have cut America's losses and left the agonizing problems of Lebanon for the Lebanese people to sort out. That would have been statesmanship, even had we arrived at the withdrawal decision late in the day.

But, with incomprehensible perverseness, the Reagan Administration made no effort whatever to extricate our country from the Lebanese morass and to formulate and pursue an independent policy tailored to our country's needs; instead it tied our country more tightly to the Begin Government's overblown ambitions as though Israel deserved an award for involving us in Lebanon.

Ever since the 1973 Yom Kippur War, Israel had been seeking to exploit America's obsession with the Soviet menace in an effort to obtain some form of defensive arrangement that would assure America's help and supplies in case of another Arab attack. In 1981, a month after the Reagan Administration had successfully resisted the efforts of the Israeli lobby to block the sale of AWACs to Saudi Arabia, the President felt compelled to compensate Israel by offering it a so-called "Strategic Cooperation Agreement." Not only would that, he hoped, appease the Israeli lobby but it would serve as payment to the Israelis for living up to their commitment to withdraw from the Sinai in accordance with the Camp David Accords—an action for which we had already paid Israel many times over.

But the kind of agreement the Administration then proposed was less than the Israelis were demanding. Israel sought some form of permanent American presence—the establishment of United States bases in Israel, the stationing of troops or at least the prepositioning of United States arms and equipment. But the Administration sought to limit cooperation to anodyne measures such as "joint maneuvers" and "joint committees." That difference in view clearly reflected the lack of common motivation for the agreement; the American desire was to improve the effectiveness of its Rapid Deployment Force which it had conceived primarily for use against Soviet aggression without disenchanting the moderate Arab states; the Israelis, on the other hand, were not haunted by the specter of an aggressive Russia but by an attack from their Arab neighbors. Thus they wanted an arrangement that would visibly symbolize America's commitment to Israel, assure that supplies would be available for sustained conflict without the need for another airlift, and, by the stationing of forces, guarantee America's immediate involvement in case of another Arab assault.

But even the watered down agreement finally agreed on never became effective, for, as has been recounted earlier, Israel suddenly seized the moment when America was deeply preoccupied with a crisis in Poland, to annex the Golan Heights. President Reagan reacted in anger by suspending the new agreement, while Prime Minister Begin, never willing to be outdone, renounced it altogether.

It will be pointed out in detail in the second part of this book why Israel and the United States do not share common objectives and why our country should be wary of tying its fortunes too closely to Israel's expansionist ambitions. But, on November 28, the Administration seemed insensitive to such inconvenient realities when it revived the proposal for a Strategic Cooperation Agreement. This time, moreover, it went much farther to meet Israel's demands, even to the point of agreeing to the prepositioning of military supplies. That meant a major loss of control for America. So long as the Israelis were compelled, in case of a protracted war, to depend on an American airlift we might, as Henry Kissinger showed in 1973, exercise some influence over Israeli actons; now we were giving that away—and for nothing.

The agreement that resulted is a classic example of a one-sided transaction. The United States extracted no concessions from Israel, and it is not clear that it tried. It did not even insist on a freeze on the construction of Israeli settlements in the occupied territories, which the American taxpayers are continuing to subsidize through our economic aid. The agreement's purpose was, the Administration piously stated, to "give priority attention to the threat to our mutual interest posed by the increased Soviet involvement in the Middle East" even though it was clear that Israel's attention was quite differently focused.

The highlights of the agreement were, as announced:

- An increase in United States military grants to Israel by $425 million annually.
- Allowing Israel to use some of this aid to build the Lavi jet fighter which it would sell in Third World markets in competition with American aircraft producers. That was strongly opposed by the American aircraft industry, and with good reason; but, although that industry regularly demonstrates formidable political clout in other contexts, it was clearly no match for the Israeli lobby. No country but Israel has ever been exempted from the settled practice of requiring military aid to be used exclusively for the purchase of American weapons. Such an exception sets a dangerous precedent.
- The establishment of a US-Israeli committee to conduct joint military exercises and arrange for the use of Israeli ports by the US Navy's Sixth Fleet
- The prepositioning of military supplies in Israel for use by the US Rapid Deployment Force—supplies that would presumably be turned over to Israel in case of attack without need for the airlift provided in 1973
- Immediate negotiations for a free trade agreement between the United States and Israel, allowing imports and exports on a duty-free and tax-free basis—concessions that will become of great value if general Third World preferences are eliminated. Whether Israel will even be held to normal subsidy rules is now in serious doubt. In any event, the Administration and the Congress seem prepared to accord Israel preferential trading arrangements it denies to our neighbor Canada.
- The resumption of shipments of US-made cluster bombs to Israel in spite of the fact that the IDF has repeatedly violated the restrictions we have placed on the use of these singularly obscene weapons.

As might have been expected, this announcement was greeted throughout the Middle East, first with incredulity, then with anger and perplexity. As Secretary Haig discovered when he sought to peddle his concept of a "strategic consensus", the Arab countries have little fear of the Soviet Union, nor has there been any "increased Soviet involvement in the Middle East". On the contrary, Russia's influence shrank enormously when Sadat expelled Soviet personnel in 1974 and, if Moscow has more activities in Syria than before 1982, it is solely because Israel forced the expansion of Russia's presence when it gratuitously smashed up Syria's Soviet-supplied equipment in the course of its Lebanese invasion.

Thus, in spite of the Administration's denials that it has any "plans for joint military planning of military actions against Syria or any other Arab country," the Arabs do not believe it. Nor should they. As they see it, the Soviet hope of increasing its influence in the Middle East will largely depend on America's failure to curb Israel and work as an honest broker in the peace process; the signing of the agreement strongly suggests that America has taken sides and disqualified itself for that role.

Why did the Administration chose to make this move at a time when our country was still paying heavily for the breakage caused by Israel's self-defeating Lebanese invasion? The simplest explanation for such masochism may be the most plausible: the decision to revive the Defense Cooperation Agreement and the timing of that decision were the reactions of officials rattled, befuddled, frustrated, feeling intense domestic political pressure, facing an election, and at a loss to know what else to do.[91] Some may suggest, in partial exculpation, that Administration strategists were influenced by Mr. Henry Kissinger's geopolitical jargon about rectifying the balance of power in the area by persuading the Israelis to resume the fight—or at least they may have recited that to one another as a rationalization for what they knew to be folly. But even on that basis, the proposal makes little sense; not only is there no indication that the balance of power has been materially affected but it is hard to see how we could improve that balance by aligning our country on the side of four million Israelis and thus making enemies of 100 million Arabs. Instead of trying to beg Israel to resume fighting we should instead be discouraging its headstrong use of military power and its misuse of our military equipment.

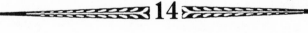

The Need for a Post Mortem

THE STORY OF ISRAEL'S INVASION OF LEBANON, of America's acquiescence and, at times, its complicity, is, as the title of this book suggests, a chronicle of error and betrayal. The errors and betrayals on the part of both the United States and Israel were not the aberrations of a moment;

they occurred throughout the whole affair with constant and humiliating regularity. Indeed they were so numerous that I have listed them in the final chapter of this book.

Meanwhile it is not enough merely to record the mistakes that have been made; if we are to salvage anything out of the flotsam and jetsam of the Lebanese shipwreck we must rigorously examine its consequences, study their significance and take to heart the lessons that vividly emerge.

That is the object of Part Two which follows—to try to assess the implications and distill the larger meaning of this foolish and tragic episode.

PART TWO

Lessons and Consequences

The Consequences of the Israeli Invasion and its Aftermath

AS I HAVE NOTED EARLIER, Lebanon is not a major player in the drama of the Middle East. It is a geographical area marked by tragedy and death, defined by an artificial boundary that contains a bizarre agglomeration of feuding factions far more possessed by tribal loyalties — by family, religion, and ethnic survival — than by any sense of nationality. The concept of Lebanon as a nation is much too fragile to bear the weight of its bloody history, and there seems little realistic possibility that it can avoid at least the *de facto* partition which has in part existed for the last eight years.

But, sad though its history — and its future — may be, Lebanon is of only minor relevance to American interests and the tragic events since June 1982 have done nothing to change that situation. Yet even if Lebanon were of transcendent importance we could still do little to shape its destiny. Israel's scheme of imposing an Israeli-influenced Maronite regime on the whole of the country was a delusion born of overweening arrogance, and the project became even less realistic once Israel had abandoned it and America had taken it over.

On balance Syria and the Islamic factions in Lebanon have gained the most by these lamentable events. President Assad has increased his stature in Middle East politics by his show of courage and astuteness, and Syria has become an active competitor with Egypt for leadership in the Arab world. The power of the Maronites is being steadily reduced to a level more nearly commensurate with their relative strength and number. Diminished by demography to the point where they are now only 20% of the Lebanese population, they have forfeited the preeminent place they occupied for so long. Nor are they any longer a consolidated political force; instead, key Maronite leaders and their militias are constantly changing their positions toward the Amin Gemayel government.

Israel is a major loser. Its record of military victories has been marred by a costly and frustrating expedition that failed in its objectives, while the Israeli people have suffered a painful blow to their excessive confidence in military might. Rather than improving Israel's security, its ill-advised military expedition has substantially increased its vulnerability. As a result of Israel's attack, the Soviet Union has now provided Syria more than $2 billion of military supplies and Israel's regional air supremacy is no longer unquestioned. The respected defense editor of *Ha'aretz*, Zeev Schiff, believes that the Syrians have already improved their ground strength to the point where they can challenge the Israeli army on the Golan Heights and from the Beka'a Valley.[92]

Not only is Israel's occupation of southern Lebanon a formidable added drain on its shattered economy (sustained only by an ever-increasing blood transfusion of American aid), but it darkens still further Israel's reputation as a democratic state, since today thirty per cent of the people under Jerusalem's rule have no right to vote. With more than one and a half million Arabs and Palestinians living under Israel's military occupation, restlessness is increasing and repression is becoming steadily more ugly. Until the invasion Israel enjoyed friendly relations with the Shiites, who are now the largest ethnic group in Lebanon; indeed grateful anti-PLO Shiites greeted the invading IDF with flowers. But now that the IDF has usurped government functions and supplanted local officials, it has become the object of hatred and violence, with the Shiites mounting an average of fifteen ambushes a week against Israeli troops.

Yet the peoples under Israeli occupation are not the only victims of its military ambitions; one must also consider those individuals and families displaced and dispersed by the IDF's conquering legions. The cumulative effect is ominous for Israel. No nation can go on acquiring more and more enemies and driving increasing masses of people into a hopeless diaspora without someday suffering a comeuppance. Wise and moderate Israelis are heartsick as their country increasingly adopts the values and psychology of a Sparta, while turning its back on the humane traditions of its founders. Those are the men and women the Administration betrayed when it gave the Begin government unquestioning support during the invasion.

If Israel is now suffering from the *hubris* of its leaders, America has lost heavily from the Reagan Administration's colossal miscalculations.

By taking sides with Israel and even making a Strategic Cooperation Agreement that is loosely referred to as an alliance, America has gravely impaired its effectiveness as a mediator and its standing with the Arab nations and peoples. By gratuitously undertaking to prop up a hopelessly weak regime in Lebanon our country has experienced a political defeat that will cost us heavily in respect and authority. By permitting itself to be tricked into breaking America's solemn promise to safeguard the Palestinians left behind when the PLO leadership departed, the Administration has cast doubt on our country's reliability and, by associating with bloody-minded factions in an internecine quarrel peripheral to its interests, it has sullied our national reputation for humanity. Finally, it has greatly enhanced the position of Syria within the Arab world and if it persists in its discriminatory arms policy it will create tempting opportunities for the Soviet Union to extend its influence.

Wise Presidents know how to admit failure, as John F. Kennedy showed following the Bay of Pigs, but President Reagan prefers to engage in Orwellian Doublespeak by fatuously claiming a Lebanese success. He would do well to recall Churchill's famous comment to the House of Commons on June 4, 1940, following the evacuation from Dunkirk: "We must be careful not to assign to this deliverance the attributes of a victory."

═══════16═══════

Lessons of Our Lebanese Experience

IF AMERICA HAS SUFFERED FOR ITS MISTAKES in Lebanon the costs might still be worthwhile if our leaders were to learn hard lessons from that experience.

Some of those lessons are of broad application, others relate specifically to the problems and dangers that confront us in the anarchic arena of the Middle East.

Lessons of Broad Application

The Reagan Administration drifted into the Lebanese imbroglio with little comprehension of, or sensitivity to, the political and social terrain on which it was venturing. Secretary Alexander Haig's vision of a non-existent "strategic consensus" contributed to the general confusion as well as the Administration's penchant for treating all issues and areas as though they were the same size and bore the same relevence to America's interests. Nor could our leaders conceal their simple faith that America's military power assured our ability to deal with every problem. Finally, the Administration's approach to Lebanon vividly illustrated the perils of defining the world predicament solely in Cold War terms.

In addition our government made other errors which it could have avoided had our leaders been more aware of history. It committed American blood and treasure to support a Lebanese regime that represented only one element in the population—repeating the mistake we made in Vietnam. It also made the egregious error of half-heartedly using American military might to try to drive out the Syrians—an objective achievable only by a major commitment of military force, involving costs and risks that our marginal interests could not possibly justify.

Above and beyond that, however, the Administration demonstrated once again our country's imperative need to learn how to disengage with minimum cost from unprofitable situations into which it may have carelessly blundered without throwing good resources after bad like an addicted gambler. The need for such a technique became urgently apparent during the Vietnamese War. Toward the latter years of the 1960s my colleagues in the high echelons of the Johnson Administration finally and reluctantly concluded—as I had from the beginning—that the United States could never achieve its avowed objectives; yet they could not face the political costs of a tactical withdrawal, which they persistently overestimated. That would, they insisted, entail a major loss of "prestige" and "credibility". How could our allies believe us, they asked, if we did not stand firm against the North Vietnamese?

My answer at the time was that our friends and allies would respect America if it showed the good sense to cut its losses and extricate itself from a situation peripheral to its interests in circumstances where it could not win. What worried me was not our failure to prevail (we could write off our losses as with any unsuccessful endeavor) but that we would not face the logic of our predicament. Yet, in spite of such advice, the President kept escalating the rhetoric and pouring in more and more young men to kill and be killed simply because no one had evolved a doctrine of extrication.

If we needed such a doctrine for our Vietnam embroilment we needed it once again in Lebanon. "All great incidents and individuals.. . occur twice," wrote Karl Marx, "the first time as tragedy, the second as farce," and Lebanon was the farcical recapitulation of Vietnam. Even after Israel had abandoned the objective with which we had imprudently associated ourselves, President Reagan continued to raise the rhetorical ante. The United States, he insisted, had a "vital interest" in Lebanon and we dare not "surrender" or "they" will "take over the whole Middle East."

The farcical aspect is that, if Lebanon was so central to our interests, why did we limit our commitment to 1800 marines backed up by gunnery practice from ships offshore when, in fulfillment of much the same rhetoric, we committed 550,000 men to Vietnam?

If, in the two situations, our deployment of force was not comparable in magnitude, our mistakes were identical. In each case our government should have acknowledged at an early point that it had erred in committing our power and prestige to support a weak government in a local conflict. It should then have moderated its rhetoric to emphasize the relative unimportance of the problem and set about seriously developing a plausible rationale for withdrawal. But, in each case, our leaders did just the opposite: they proclaimed with increasingly shrill hyperbole the indispensability of an unattainable victory and the catastrophic consequences of an inevitable defeat. In Vietnam, as a consequence, we lost 55,000 dead, while in Lebanon we left our beleaguered Marines in a position of hopeless frustration, exposed to cross-fire in a conflict in which their country had only a minor interest.

Although the Reagan Administration should have learned these lessons of general application from our Lebanese fiasco there seems little evidence that it has done so. We now seem to be making the same movie all over again; only slightly rewriting the script to insert Latin American place names, but displaying the same style and mannerisms based on the same misconceptions—an overblown assessment of the area's importance; an exaggerated belief in its Cold War relevence; a blind disregard of political, social and economic realities; and a childlike faith in military solutions.

Lessons Regarding the Middle East

If, on the evidence so far, our government—and indeed our country—seems to have learned little of general application from the folly of our Lebanon intervention, has that experience made it wiser with regard to the tangled and menacing problems of the Middle East and particularly our relations with Israel which lie at the heart of our Middle East plight? That is the central question Americans should be pondering today, for the Middle East is beyond question the most dangerous area in the world; it is, as I shall show, the potential Balkans of World War III.

What the preceding pages have told us is that the United States blundered into Lebanon because, possessing no Middle East policy of its own, it blindly reacted to Israeli policies designed to achieve objectives that contravened our interests. To save ourselves from even more dangerous and destructive ventures we should be quite clear as to the nature and effect of our current relations with Israel and examine with care and rigor where they are leading us.

I shall, in the remaining pages, consider how our relations with Israel have evolved in recent years, the false assumptions that now underlie those relations, the dangers inherent in the prospective evolution of events if we remain on our present course, and the urgent need for us to redesign United States-Israeli relations on a mutually self-respecting basis if we are to avoid the disasters toward which both of our nations are currently—and rapidly—drifting.

The Issue of Responsibility

First, as a prelude to the larger discussion, let me clarify the issue of responsibility.

In discussing the events that followed Israel's invasion of Lebanon I have concentrated primarily on Israeli policies and actions because the Reagan Administration did little more than react to Israeli initiatives. Yet I do not suggest that all troubles in the Middle East are solely the result of Israeli obduracy or ambition or even of American miscalculation and flaccidity. Certainly the Arabs must bear their share of the blame.

Throughout the Arab world, to an extraordinary degree, intellectual habits and objective facts are out of joint; political ideas have not kept pace with events nor have the attitudes of rival factions and nations evolved in phase. As a result many Arab leaders have, at least until recently, persistently rejected reality. Immobilized by exaggerated pride, embittered by defeat and exile, bemused by animosity and wishful thinking, they have substituted flamboyant rhetoric for rational and effective action.

At a time when the Arab states might have accepted the State of Israel as a permanent political fact and made peace, they fought, were repeatedly defeated, and retreated into a protracted period of surly and ineffectual rejectionism. It was poignant irony that, at the Fez Conference in 1982, they belatedly conceded the reality of Israel, yet offered only what the Israelis would have gladly accepted in 1949. Yet by then, Israel's expectations had expanded extravagantly and in America a strong and disciplined pro-Israeli pressure group disabled our country from even attempting to bridge the gap.

Nor has the Arabs' failure to face reality or consult their true interests been their only contribution to the current disastrous confusion. By insisting on decision by consensus while lacking unity of purpose, the Arab nations have permitted extremist states such as Libya and South Yemen to impose a veto on their decisions. Thus, with the irrationality that pervades the Middle East, those Arab nations that suffered the costs and casualties of fighting Israel have let their policies be dictated by those that shirked the battle.

Finally, one must fault the Arabs for failing to assist the Palestinians in any effective—or even humane—way. Although they talk with eloquence and passion about the tragic Palestinian plight, they have left those victimized peoples to improvise their own defense through the PLO. Yet the PLO has suffered from the same debilitating weakness as the Arab League. It too depends on consensus and reflects in microcosm the same divergence of opinions. Thus it has been disabled by disunity from taking other than extreme positions that preclude productive participation in the search for peace.

The Arabs, in short, have been left by their own indecisiveness in a posture of no war and no peace; their language is bellicose, but their actions spasmodic and half-hearted. They have condoned terrorist attacks, but the radical Arab states that protect the terrorists have shunned open warfare. Many Arab leaders have called rhetorically for peace, yet have repeatedly failed to grasp chances for peace when they may have been briefly available.

Thus we are once again confronted by a pattern repeated monotonously in history—the tragic predicament of two rival peoples misled by willful but weak leaders without vision—too self-indulgent to look beyond the fleeting moment, too filled with hatred, greed and false pride to face reality, and too timid to make peace.

Just as the American government and Israel's American supporters, by indiscriminately supporting expansionist Israeli governments, habitually play into the hands of Israeli hardliners, many of the Arab nations strengthen those same hardliners by failing to propose their own peace initiatives or to support United States initiatives. They demand instead that Washington save them from the consequences of their disunity and inactivity by bringing the Israelis to heel.

Israel's supporters, on the other hand, insist that the United States wring concessions from the Arabs but never, never put pressure on Israel. Why, they ask, should America not force the Arabs to meet Israel's conditions? But the practical answer to that contention is obvious. The United States has relatively little leverage on the Arab nations because it provides them few benefits. On the other hand, America maintains Israel's standard of living, supplies it with massive arms, and runs political interference for it. As fully described in the first part of this book, our country has enormous leverage with Israel; all it lacks is the will to use it.

If there is to be peace in the Middle East—which seems increasingly unlikely—it will be only because America begins to use its leverage with Israel while it still has some residue of influence with the other side. But that may be only a fleeting moment, for, as will be pointed out, the smotheringly close identification with Israel toward which our country is moving will soon destroy any remaining influence with the Arabs and encourage the radicalization of the moderate Arab nations.

The 1967 War and the Progressive Degradation of American Middle East Policy

AMERICA'S INVOLVEMENT in the Middle East has been marked by a gradual retrogression from neutrality to partisanship. Beginning with the establishment of the State of Israel in 1948 and lasting until the Six-Day War of 1967, the United States tried (with occasional lapses), to act as an impartial referee between the combatants in the Middle East arena, exercising political and economic persuasion to try to promote reconciliation and maintain the peace.

That was obviously the appropriate role for a superpower with diverse interests in the area and an overwhelming interest in peace. Thus in 1950 the United States refused Israel's request to sell it arms; instead, to avoid encouraging an arms race, our government sought to coordinate arms sales with Britain and France through the Tripartite Declaration of May 25, 1950.

Thereafter, until the end of the Kennedy Administration, that Declaration remained a central tenet of American Middle Eastern policy, with our government earnestly seeking to maintain some degree of objectivity in formulating Middle East policy. America sought, so far as practicable, to be even-handed on the assumption that peace could be best assured by maintaining a rough arms balance in the area.

But under the Johnson Administration, American support for Israel began to change both qualitatively and quantitatively. United States government's assistance to Israel in the fiscal year 1964, the last budget year of the Kennedy Administration, amounted to $40 million, virtually none of which was military. Then Lyndon Johnson turned his back on the policy of even-handedness and ignored the Tripartite Declaration. In the fiscal years 1965 and 1966, his Administration provided Israel not merely with defensive weapons but also with 250 tanks and 48 attack aircraft. So rapid was the inflation of our aid that, in the fiscal year 1966 alone, we provided more military assistance to Israel than we had cumulatively provided during all the years since its establishment as a nation.

Such an abrupt departure from a heretofore coherent and bipartisan U.S. foreign policy was a radical change. Yet the aid level attained in

1966 was only a dim presage of things to come, for, after the 1967 war, both our military and economic aid shot precipitously upward, as President Johnson, responding to domestic pressures and the urging of political friends, transformed the fundamental American-Israeli politico-military relationship. For the first time, America became Israel's primary arms supplier, economic benefactor and political supporter, as a torrent of U.S. money and military materiel began flowing to Israel.

The Six-Day War of 1967 — A Watershed

The 1967 War was a critical turning point in America's relations with Israel. Not only did it drastically increase the degree, and even the nature, of Israel's dependence on America but it turned a principled relationship into one unhealthy for both sides. Not only did America repudiate the concept of an arms balance and become Israel's principal weapons supplier, but a succession of American Governments abandoned the firm and wise policy President Eisenhower had enunciated in 1956 that aggressors should not be allowed to keep the lands they conquer by force or impose conditions on the restoration of those lands.

The departure from principle began in the aftermath of the 1967 war, during which Israel occupied the West Bank including East Jerusalem, as well as the Golan Heights and the Gaza Strip. In the haggling that followed, the United Nations Security Council adopted Resolution 242 which contemplated the exchange of seized territories for peace. However, in deference to Israel the territories to be returned were defined ambiguously while the resolution also omitted any time limits or guidelines for withdrawal or any explicit provision for self-determination by the Palestinian peoples displaced or under occupation. As a result it laid the basis for a protracted stalemate during which positions have hardened on both sides. Curiously, the Israeli Government's formal agreement to the Resolution was never obtained, a technicality that has allowed succeeding governments to claim they are not bound by it, even though no objections were offered at the time.

Since the Arabs declined to negotiate from a position of humiliation when they felt their bargaining power inadequate and the Israelis refused to talk with the PLO, which the Arab League had designated as the exclusive spokesman for the Palestinians, no negotiations occurred. Instead, the Arab nations began reluctantly to rebuild their armies to bring their military competence more nearly in line with their incendiary language; Egypt turned to the Russians for arms while the United States increased its grants and military assistance to Israel.

Donald Neff, in his recently published and highly perceptive book,

Warriors for Jerusalem, has described the insidious consequences of the 1967 war in vivid terms:

> . . . the war of 1967 was the worst tragedy in the modern history of the Middle East. In the sixteen years since then, the region has been racked by more hatred, violence and bloodshed than at any time since the founding of the Jewish state. The mere listing of the major events makes a doleful litany: the war of attrition, Black September, the PLO terror campaign culminating in the Munich massacre, the traumatic 1973 war, the struggle for southern Lebanon that led to the near destruction of Beirut and, once again, the massacre and uprooting of thousands of Palestinian refugees leading to renewed hatred.[93]

One major consequence of the 1967 war was to make America Israel's number one arms supplier. But, if that war, which excited Johnson's pro-Israeli sympathies, resulted in an abrupt and dramatic escalation in American aid, the levels reached were still modest compared with the astronomical magnitudes of assistance provided after the 1973 war by the Nixon Administration. Then, in the course of Henry Kissinger's breathless shuttling, America in practical terms bought peace between Israel and Egypt. The settlement was an Alice-in-Wonderland type of real estate transaction: the United States, in effect, purchased thousands of square miles of sand from the Israelis for an exorbitant sum, then paid the Egyptians an exorbitant sum to take it back.

But that was only the down payment, for, evolving from the Kissinger diplomacy was a pattern of ever-increasing levels of aid, including military assistance, that would make Israel by far the most powerful military nation in the Middle East—to the point where today it is, as the Israelis themselves frequently boast, the fourth strongest military power in the world.

The table that follows explicitly tells the story for it shows how—both before and after the Yom Kippur War, the Nixon Administration accelerated the flow so that, since the mid-1960s, U.S. aid to Israel, both military and economic, has increased by several orders of magnitude. For example, as the table shows, U.S. military aid to Israel for the thirteen years from 1948 to 1961 amounted to less than one million dollars; then, in the twenty-two years from 1962 through 1984, that military aid figure rose to a cumulative total of over $18 billion.

The evolution of American aid to Israel is shown by the following table:

AMERICAN AID TO ISRAEL
(Millions of Dollars)

Dates	Military		Economic		Combined	
	Total	Avg/Yr	Total	Avg/Yr	Total	Avg/Yr
1948-61	$ .9	(*)	$ 593.6	$ 42.4	$ 594.5	$ 42.5
1962-73	3,911.6	$ 300.9	713.7	54.9	4,624,3	355.7
1974-78	4,000.0	800.0	2,679.9	536.0	6,679.9	1,336.0
1979-84	11,500.0	1,916.7	4,931.1	821.9	16,431.1	2,738.5
	19,412.5		8,918.3		28,329.8	

(*) Less than $100,000 per year.

The rapid escalation of aid during the period 1979-1984 has occurred despite the Camp David Accords which, by neutralizing Egypt, should have reduced Israel's military requirements. The cost of purchasing Egyptian support for those agreements—an indirect subsidy for Israel—has been in excess of $10 billion. Thus, if both costs are combined, the Israeli-Egyptian peace has cost America a total of $25 billion in subsidies or over $4 billion per year since 1979, and the costs are still escalating. Our government loans to Israel are for 30-year terms, whereas we hold other countries to 13-year terms. If the Israeli lobby succeeds in its current efforts most, if not all, of the present $9 billion of loans will be written off. The Defense Department considers the military threat to Israel as being far less severe than does Israel.[94]

The Rationale for Arming Israel

To justify the drastic increase of our aid to Israel following the 1967 war, America reversed the policy assumptions under which that aid was provided. Yielding to political pressure it no longer contended that Middle East peace could best be secured by maintaining an arms balance; instead, Israel should be provided with arms and equipment surpassing that of all its Arab neighbors.

The rationale for thus turning policy on its head was compounded of casuistry, wishful thinking, and domestic politics. So long as Israel continued to feel insecure, it would, its supporters argued, be reluctant to pursue peace initiatives; but once we assured it arms supremacy, a relaxed Israel would be cooperative and forthcoming in seeking peace with its neighbors. No one bothered to ask what effect an over-armed Israel might have on the policies of the Arab states or whether it would serve American interests to fuel a Middle East arms race.

In any event, developments since 1973 have shown that rationalization to be dangerously misleading. Instead of encouraging compromise and accommodation, Israel's growing confidence in its military superiority has led it to reject settlement proposals even more vehemently than had previously been the case.[*]

Henry Kissinger summarized the Israeli attitude when he wrote with regard to the then Israeli Prime Minister, "I ask Rabin to make concessions, and he says he can't because Israel is weak. So I give him more arms,and he says he doesn't need to make concessions because Israel is strong."[95]

Yet Kissinger could hardly have been surprised by Rabin's attitude; he had himself, some years earlier, expounded a principle that explained why, no matter how excessively we armed Israel, the Israelis would resist the concessions necessary for peace:

> Whenever there exists a power which considers the international order . . . oppressive, relations between it and other powers will be revolutionary. . . . To be sure, the motivation of the revolutionary power may well be defensive; it may well be sincere in its protestations of feeling threatened. But the distinguishing feature of a revolutionary power is not that it feels threatened — such feeling is inherent in the nature of international relations based on sovereign states — but that nothing can reassure it. Only absolute security — the neutralization of the opponent — is considered a sufficient guarantee, and thus the desire of one power for absolute security means absolute insecurity for all the others.
>
> Diplomacy, the art of restraining the exercise of power, cannot function in such an environment.[96] (underlining supplied)

Israel is still formally at war with all its neighbors except Egypt and its neuroses are now so far advanced that no amount of military power can provide it the "absolute security" it desires; thus it inevitably seeks "the neutralization" of its opponents as the only "sufficient guarantee". In Middle East politics Israel is thus, in Kissinger's terms, a "revolu-

---

(*) American policy bears a heavy load of blame for the failure to resolve the bitter problems of the area. After the 1973 war, in which the Arabs exorcised their earlier shame by an unexpected show of valor and competence,the United States might, by an even-handed and continuous application of pressure, have achieved a major breakthrough toward a comprehensive peace. That was, of course, what Sadat had wanted in his historic pilgrimage to Jerusalem — and indeed what President Carter earnestly sought to achieve. But Carter grew weary of beating against the gneiss of Begin's obduracy while the Likud government relentlessly pursued its own strategic plan. By agreeing at Camp David to a bilateral settlement with Egypt (for which he exacted another exorbitant payment from the United States) Begin achieved a long-held objective of effectively neutralizing the largest power in the Arab world; then, no longer threatened by a two-front attack, he felt free to ignore his equivocal commitment to the second phase of the Camp David Accords. Israel would, Prime Minister Begin fiercely said, give up not one inch of the West Bank, while, as mentioned earlier, he exploited a moment when America was preoccupied with Poland to annex the Golan Heights.

Since then the United States has made several half-hearted gestures toward resolving the Palestinian issue. But the Israelis have exploited Arab disunity to stall any serious move toward negotiation, assured by the demonstrated virtuosity of their zealous American friends to believe that the United States Congress could be induced to finance their settlements policy long enough to foreclose any serious danger of negotiation.

tionary power", and, under those circumstances, "diplomacy, the art of restraining the exercise of power, cannot function."

If America has been wrong in assuming that an overarmed Israel would feel secure and hence amenable to peacemaking, many Israelis—including some who shape government policy—were, at least until recently, proceeding on an equally mistaken assumption. They nourished the wishful thought that Israel's Arab neighbors would ultimately become reconciled to the reality of Israel's overwhelming power and accept its expanded boundaries as a *fait accompli*. As with other assumptions born of desire rather than logic, such a comforting belief runs counter to experience and even more to the long memories that complicate Middle East politics. If Israeli policy is overlain with the mystique of the Promised Land—a title deed four thousand years old—Israel's neighbors are also haunted by history. To them Israel is an intruder—a "neo Philistine" state which, like ancient Philistia before it, is made up of migrants to the region, supported from abroad and seeking domination and conquest through superior might and a program of settlements in the Judean hill country.

The alarm induced by the spectacle of ever-increasing Israeli military power is not leading the Arab nations to accept the *status quo*; on the contrary it is gradually overcoming the Arabs' lethargy and compelling their governments to prepare for an eventual showdown. Israel gave added impetus to that process by attacking Syria and humiliating its Soviet patron; Syria has replied by a major arms build-up that is, in turn, stimulating Israeli demands for more and more arms. Unless the arms race can be halted, there is little possibility of diplomacy through negotiation, leaving only what Clausewitz referred to as "diplomacy by other means"—or, in other words, a disastrous war that could very well involve the United States.

I find no basis for believing that the Arab nations will become gradually reconciled to Israel's current boundaries; on the contrary, as a result of their Lebanese adventure and their occupation of south Lebanon, the Israelis have added substantially to the number of their enemies. So long as Syria sees Israel's annexation of the Golan heights as a threat to its security, so long as three million Palestinians scattered throughout the Arab world continue to agitate for a homeland, and so long as Israel continues the process of dispossessing and repressing the occupants of the West Bank and especially so long as the IDF remains in southern Lebanon, renewed war seems inevitable. Indeed a protracted state of war is assured so long as Israel continues to pursue its compulsive search for "defensible borders" through conquest and occupation. Napoleon tragically demonstrated the folly of such a concept when he ravaged Europe for fifteen years in the effort to achieve the French Revolution's goal of "natural frontiers." Today, as many Israelis are beginning to recognize, Israel's settlements on the West Bank do not improve but diminish its security. Those settlements are singularly vulnerable to enemy guns, rockets and armies, while far from securing Israel's borders, the presence of the settlers could only add to civilian casualty lists.

Today America can no longer afford a policy of acquiescent diplomacy for we are rapidly losing the diplomatic middle ground. The Arabs did not turn toward the United States after the 1973 war out of affection for us or dislike of the Soviets; they saw our country as the only power that possessed effective leverage with the Israelis and thus the only power with the ability to secure the return of their territories without further conflict. But that attitude is rapidly changing, as America becomes more and more hostage to Israeli whims and ambitions. If, as many are now urging, we make a full-fledged alliance with Israel, America will have become the Arabs' enemy. Meanwhile, as they watch United States' impotence in dealing with an importunate Israel, the Arab nations are being driven once more to pursue a war policy that only the Soviet Union is prepared to support.

The prime lesson for America is that, in the Middle East, time works against peace. Most of today's key Arab rulers are pragmatists — dealers in the art of the possible. They can still be brought to a settlement if America insists that Israel abandon its obsession as a "revolutionary power" with "absolute security". But little time is left. If current trends continue, the Arab rulers of the future will be more doctrinaire, more determined and far less susceptible to American influence.

Growing Strength of the Israeli Lobby and the Move Toward Polarization

Because time is working against peace it seems particularly lamentable that serious peace initiatives should be impeded if not foreclosed by the institutionalized paralysis of American politics — a steadily increasing development over the last twenty-eight years. Outraged and alarmed by Eisenhower's principled insistence in 1956 that Israel return the territories it had seized in the six-day Suez war, American Jewish leaders promptly set about marshalling their formidable political resources to achieve unique power and effectiveness. Had they focused that political clout on encouraging and assisting Israel to seek peace, they might have transformed the anguished face of the Middle East; but instead they have uncritically supported and defended every action and policy of whatever Israeli government happened to be in power.

Particularly since the Likud Party gained control of the government, their indiscriminate support has tended to undercut the moderate Israeli elements they should be encouraging.

Without intending that result, the Israeli lobby has strengthened the Begins and Sharons and Shamirs who have been leading Israel down a self-destructive course. By using its political power to assure that Israel is armed *cap-a-pied*, and, at the same time, obstructing the sale of American arms to moderate Arab states, it is forcing Arab governments to move politically away from America and to turn to suppliers less friendly to Israel.

The inevitable result of such pressure, if continued, will be to polarize the tangled politics of the Middle East, leaving the United States, as Israel's only champion, increasingly alienated from even the most moderate Arab states. As a result, those Arab nations will inevitably be pushed toward an accelerating militarization, a reluctant accommodation with the more extreme Arab regimes, and an increasing dependence on the Soviet Union for arms and military supplies.

⟨18⟩

The Ripening Fruits of Polarization

THE BITTER FRUITS OF THAT PRESSURE TOWARD POLARIZATION were clearly apparent in two interviews which King Hussein of Jordan gave in March 1984. In those interviews the King characterized the United States as disqualified by its increasingly one-sided approach from any longer playing a role of mediator in the Arab-Israeli conflict. Although Israel's American supporters treated his comments with scornful disparagement, his interviews merely made explicit what has long been evident to competent observers. Impelled by a fatal mixture of innocence and indecision, the United States is, so the King implied, assisting Israel to polarize the Middle East. Without a change in American policy—and he despairs of such a change—he sees no hope for the reversal of that trend—nor do I. Thoughtful Americans should carefully ponder his comments, for they reveal the bitter fruits of the polarization that has already resulted from the policies America has been persuaded to follow by the Israeli government and America's Israeli lobby. His two interviews may well be noted in the history books as marking a major step toward the collapse of any hopes for peace in the Middle East.[97]

There is no mystery about the timing of the King's statement. When he spoke in March he could clearly discern the basic forces and trends in American politics. He saw America's political leaders undergoing the squalid indignities of an election year with candidates for President and members of Congress approaching the bounds of lunacy to demonstrate their subservience to the Israeli lobby. He was aware—as both he and President Mubarak of Egypt made clear—that, having blocked the sale of Stinger anti-aircraft missiles to his country, many in Congress favored legitimatizing Israel's annexation of East Jerusalem by moving the American Embassy to Jerusalem, even though that would insult and infuriate the 600 million adherents to Islam for whom Jerusalem is a sacred city third only to Mecca and Medina.

Although the Reagan Administration undertook to try to deflect such Congressional mischief, there was no assurance it could do so; moreover, the President carelessly embarrassed the King when he implied, in addressing a dinner sponsored by the Young Leadership Conference of the United Jewish Appeal, that any arms sales to Jordan would be negotiated with the Israeli lobby—a position which made his acceptance of such weapons unacceptably humiliating.

That, however, was only the most recent episode in an arid season of disillusion. After President Reagan's peace proposals on September 1, 1982, our government had called on the King to join in negotiations under the Camp David umbrella. When the King tried but failed to gain a mandate for such participation from key Palestinian elements, Israel's American supporters accused him of sabotaging the President's initiative. They conveniently overlooked the following facts:

1. From the outset the Israeli government flatly rejected the Reagan Plan and Prime Minister Begin stated categorically that Israel would never return any of the captured territory, thereby giving the King no incentive to enter talks.

2. In spite of the President's futile call for a moratorium on settlements the United States continued to subsidize Israel's expanding settlements program and even vetoed a United Nations Resolution that declared it illegal. Meanwhile, as the King pointed out, not only is Israel's occupation of the West Bank increasingly repressive,[*] but the settlements program is rapidly approaching the point of no return.

(*) A new decree mandates up to 20 years imprisonment for even throwing a rock at a vehicle whether anyone or anything is hit or not. *The Jerusalem Post* (International Edition), 3-10 June 1984, p. 5.

3. In his September 1 proposal the President ruled out the creation of a separate Palestinian state, insisting on the so-called Jordanian solution. Despite the fact that that solution had been universally rejected by Arab leaders in the West Bank, Hussein still tried to obtain the approval of Palestinian leaders for an acceptable formula for Palestinian representation. As he explained to the President on his visit to Washington, he would need to consult with, and gain the consent of, the 300-man Palestine National Council and particularly the 160 members of the Council resident in the West Bank and the Gaza Strip. But the Israelis blocked such consultation by denying exit visas that would allow the West Bank and Gaza Strip leaders to go to Jordan to meet with the King. When the King then asked for help, President Reagan refused to press the Israelis to reverse that decision.[98]

To be sure, the Administration insists that it promised Hussein that, if he would only announce his willingness to negotiate with Israel, America would *try* to use its influence to persuade the Israelis to halt their settlements program. But, in view of America's failure over the past decade to achieve even a brief moratorium on settlements, or even to reduce the American subsidy that finances that program, how could the King trust such a vague promise sufficiently to risk humiliation in the Arab world if—as seems almost certain— America would once again fail to act effectively? The King can count the votes in Congress and he has good reason to doubt that the Reagan Administration would be able, even if it tried, to impose a moratorium on settlements or even to stop subsidizing them. As the King well knows, the issue is not one of partisan politics; the Democratic presidential candidates have appeared —at least in their rhetoric—even more frantic than President Reagan to appease Israel's supporters.

Meanwhile, the King interprets Israel's systematic efforts to relocate West Bank Palestinians to the Jordan valley as "what appears . . . to be a final step toward pushing them across the river, consistent with (the Israeli's) claim that the Palestinian problem is a problem of people, not land." And, in addition, he takes note of "a plan to implement Israeli land laws on the rest of the occupied territories."(*)

That then is King Hussein's definitive assessment of the situation as he sees it. But what are the larger implications of the King's sad conclusions?

(*) The importance of the Israeli land laws is that *all* land is owned by the State or the Jewish Trust both of which possess the right of eminent domain so that the Arabs can be driven out of their country as trespassers. Such laws have been enforced even against Israeli Arab citizens; non-citizens are in an even more hopeless situation.

As has been suggested in the earlier pages, Israeli extremists, such as General Sharon, have long wanted to bring about the overthrow of King Hussein, since, in Sharon's view, that would justify Israel in attacking a radicalized Palestinian state and dominating it by force. Nor is that merely Sharon's idiosyncratic scheme; it is shared by the Shamir government's more extreme leaders. Roni Milo, the head of the Likud bloc in the Knesset (to which both Begin and Shamir belong), stated in a recent Knesset debate that the party had not abandoned its claim to the East Bank (the whole of Jordan), which they call "Eastern Eretz Yisrael", although they *might* do so as part of a negotiated settlement with Jordan.[99]

Such irresponsible talk in Israel is doubly mischievous; it not only encourages extremists to dream of recreating the empires of David and Solomon, it also gives credence to the widely held belief in military circles that, in the event of a war with Syria, the IDF would attack through northern Jordan. Such a strategy is made increasingly plausible by current Soviet efforts to help the Syrians complete impressive fortifications opposite the Golan Heights. To outflank that new Maginot Line and thus save unacceptable casualties, the IDF would be forced to attack through Jordan even though Jordan wished to remain neutral in the Israeli-Syrian struggle.

All this the King finds acutely upsetting. For many years he has pursued policies designed to avoid war. He has devoted available funds more to development projects than to armament, and, as a result, Jordan's military forces have fallen proportionately behind its neighbors. But, now that the King has lost faith that America will deter Israeli adventures, he is increasingly pressed to expand his armed forces with, if necessary, Soviet weapons.

That expansion is now under way with the announcement that the King is planning to increase the size of his regular army and to create a 200,000 "peoples militia" after the Iraqi model; he is also undertaking to strengthen his relations with Syria and the PLO, and turning to Moscow for military hardware. There have recently been reports of high-level Jordanian delegations traveling to Damascus for talks with President Assad, while political talks are continuing with Vladimir Boliakov, head of Mid-East Affairs in the Soviet Foreign Ministry, who has been visiting in Amman. Moreover, government sources in Amman reported early in August that Jordan's Chief of Staff was planning a trip to Moscow to buy more sophisticated weaponry. As the cumulative result of a long series of disappointments and reversals, the King has at long last concluded that Jordan can no longer count on the United States as a source of supply, while the Soviets are apparently promising more attractive payment terms than Western Europe. In addition, there are rumors that the King may also be seeking economic aid from the Soviet Union.[100]

Even little Kuwait, prevented by our government from purchasing Stinger anti-aircraft missiles to defend its oil, has now felt forced to make a deal with the Soviet Union for $327 million of surface-to-air and surface-to-surface missiles, tanks and other military materiel. One can expect this practice to spread with more and more Arab nations enlarging their armed forces and reequipping them from the Soviet arsenal.

As the Arab states increasingly lose faith in America, more and more are concluding that only by force can they recover such strategic points as the Golan Heights or find a homeland for Palestinians now in the diaspora or break the rule of Israel over one-and-a-half million Palestinians and over other Arabs in the occupied areas, which now include southern Lebanon. They know all too well that Israel has never surrendered Arab territory unless compelled to do so by outside pressure (Suez in 1956); when confronted by a tactical need to buy off a dangerous opponent (Egypt in 1979); or when faced with unacceptably high casualties (Lebanon in 1983). Thus, with Syria rapidly improving its military might with Soviet help, and other Eastern Arab states expanding and improving their armed forces, the Israeli future is necessarily uneasy. Some military experts are beginning to predict that, probably in 1988 or 1989, if diplomacy remains on dead center, key Arab nations may achieve a level of force strength and armaments sufficient to encourage them to resolve their struggle with Israel through military means.

19

The Implications of an American Security Guarantee to Israel

ALL THIS IS FORCING SOME WORRIED ISRAELIS and their American friends to question two fundamental assumptions that have at least subconsciously influenced the policies of the Israeli government. The first is the belief, which I have previously mentioned, that the Arab states, whom they perceive as technically incompetent and unable to unite on a common and consistent policy, would ultimately grow tired of fighting with Israel and reconcile themselves to the permanence of

Israel's current extended borders. But events are beginning to shake that assumption, giving way to a greater realism. Many recall that Egypt began preparations for the 1973 Yom Kippur War immediately after the Six Day War in 1967 and fears are beginning to emerge that Israel's Arab neighbors, presumably led by Syria, may within a few years feel strong enough to undertake once again to recover their conquered territories by force.

The second assumption now beginning to be challenged is that, with Egypt neutralized by Camp David, and the United States assuring a steady flow of money, weapons, and equipment, Israel could continue indefinitely to maintain its military dominance. But here again the canker of doubt is at work and some are beginning to worry that, stimulated by the Lebanese invasion to undertake greatly intensified rearmament efforts, Israel's Arab neighbors may for the first time be able to field forces equal to, or exceeding, the IDF in number and approaching it in competence.

Unhappily these disturbing thoughts are not inspiring the new skeptics to intensify the search for peace while it is still possible. Nor are they urging America to develop closer relations with Israel's neighboring Arab states, thus increasing its influence on the side of restraint. On the contrary, Israel and its American friends seem bent on weakening US-Arab relations, both as a step to, and a result of, solidifying the exclusive character of America's ties with Israel.

All this foretells a break with the past. For years Israeli leaders have proudly boasted that given the tools, Israel could defend itself by its own efforts and that their country would never ask for the intervention of a single American soldier; indeed Israelis seemed genuinely wary of too close a tie with the United States that might compromise Israel's freedom of action and maneuver. But in the post-Lebanon *tristesse,* there are increasing signs of a shift in mood and policy. Thus today many are beginning to agitate for a formal commitment that American forces would always be available and even that a significant American presence might be permanently maintained.

The glibness with which American politicians ritually assure Israel that America will protect its security has largely derived from the belief that, so long as it is supplied and equipped by America, Israel will never need to call on America's armed forces, and a similar belief seems to underly much of the casual discussion of a formal American security commitment. The unstated assumption is that the integrity of that commitment would never be tested because the very fact of America's involvement should be sufficient to deter any Arab attack.

But such an assumption is unproved, and, particularly in the light of recent events, it should not be accepted cavalierly, for it reflects a critical misconception of the dynamics of Middle East politics. Not only are Arab military decisions often influenced as much by passion as logic, but, once the United States were to join Israel as its ally—and hence the Arabs' enemy, the result would be far more likely to speed the radicalization of Arab nations and to push them toward the Soviets than to deter them from military action.

Nor does experience suggest that the Arab states are in deadly fear of the United States. President Assad of Syria seemed quite willing to call the American bluff in Lebanon; he did not back down even when the battleship New Jersey began wildly shooting its sixteen-inch guns at Syrian outposts. If, as seems likely, his willingness to defy America was influenced by his awareness of America's domestic perturbations and the reluctance of either the Administration or the Congress to commit American forces to the turbulent Middle East, that same reluctance could prove an even more influential factor were America called on to send troops to Israel.

As The Arab Nations Expand And Improve Their Military Competence It Will Be Difficult, If Not Impossible, For The IDF To Defend Israel Without American Intervention

The prospect of further war raises two disturbing questions. First, how far can Israel go in gratifying its territorial ambitions without creating such pressures on Egypt as to force it to renounce its peace arrangements? And, second, even if Egypt holds firm to its Camp David commitments, how long, if existing trends continue, will Israel's manpower resources prove sufficient to enable it to resist attack from its other Arab neighbors without the need for American military intervention?

There is no doubt that Egypt would like to remain at peace with Israel, yet, if current trends continue, the longevity of that peace cannot be counted on.

Sadat made an accord with Israel on the assumption that the second phase of Camp David would be carried out—or, at least, that there would be serious negotiations to resolve the problem of the occupied areas—and particularly the West Bank. By rejecting such negotiations, by preempting the land and water supply of the West Bank through its settlements program, by annexing the Golan Heights, and by attacking two Arab governments, Lebanon and Syria, Israel has greatly embarrassed Egypt's relations with the rest of the Arab world.

Under these circumstances how long will Egypt be content to remain estranged from other Arab nations? It has already shown its desire to regain Arab respectability by moving on January 13, 1984, to secure readmission to the Organization for the Islamic Conference. If Israel should again become involved in an attack on an Arab neighbor such as Syria or Jordan, even America's massive annual subsidy could not guarantee the durability of the Camp David arrangements; Egypt could always turn for financial help to the oil-rich Arab countries.

Even if Egypt remains neutral in the conflict, Israel's military posture will weaken in relative terms. There are several reasons why the trend toward polarization is undercutting the premises on which Israel bases its defense.

Israel's past successes have been, to a large degree, due to its extraordinary efficiency in mobilizing and concentrating its forces. The prevailing image of Israel as David against the Arab Goliath is a sentimental myth; in fact, because of Arab incompetence and disunity, Israel has, in every war so far, been able, in spite of its small population, to deploy more men in actual combat than have its combined Arab antagonists. That point is illustrated by the following table:[101]

	Arab Participants		Israeli Participants
Year	Nominal	Actual	Actual
1948	90,000	33,000	50,000
1956	275,000	150,000	225,000
1967	475,000	290,000	375,000
1973	600,000	450,000	500,000

In this table the second column shows, for each war, the size of the Arab forces that were actually committed in combat with Israel in addition to trainees and presumably mobilizable reserves.

Although the first column shows the total listed armed strength of the Arab nations (including Egypt) that were officially at war with Israel, only a limited number of those nations actually sent troops to the battle. Even those nations engaging in the fight committed only a portion of their total forces, either because they were occupied elsewhere (as was Egypt in North Yemen in 1967) or because of internal political problems (Syria in 1967). But that is changing. As has been earlier pointed out, the attack on Syria during Israel's Lebanese invasion, has, by increasing Soviet commitments to Syria, greatly increased the effectiveness of Syrian arms. Thus even should Egypt remain out of the fray, it could be only a question of time until Israel was compelled, for the first time, to face forces more numerous than its own.

By the end of the current year, 1984, Israel should probably be able to marshall about 675,000 personnel; its opponents could muster the following forces: Syria—500,000; Jordan—100,000; Palestinian Guerrillas—10,000; Saudi Arabia, Lebanon and other smaller states—10,000; making a total of 620,000. (That figure assumes not only that the peace with Egypt continues to hold, but that all other states now formally at war with Israel, such as Morocco, Algeria, Tunisia, Libya, Iraq, The Sudan, and the Gulf States would send purely token forces, if any at all.) Were Iraq to extricate itself from its current involvement with Iran and overcome its long-continuing internecine Ba'athist feud with Syria, it should be in position to provide a substantial number of combat-hardened troops to friendly Jordan. In addition, the figure for Syria is almost certainly understated since President Assad has only recently announced a mobilization scheme calling for 800,000 troops by the end of 1985.

Thus the balance sheet by early 1986 could well show 700,000 for Israel arrayed against Arab forces (still excluding Egypt) totalling 1,335,000—composed of:

Syria	800,000
Jordan	220,000
Iraq	250,000
The Gulf States	40,000
Palestinians	10,000

In 1956 and 1967 Israel benefitted heavily by the factor of surprise, but Egypt's crossing of the Nile in 1973 demonstrated that that advantage may not always be on Israel's side. At the same time, a continuance of intensive Soviet training of Syria's forces could presage a gradual narrowing of the gap in military competence. Finally, were peace with Egypt ever to break down under the strains of a renewed Arab-Israeli conflict, Israel might be outnumbered by about 3 to 1. While even that would not guarantee an Arab victory, it would make an Arab defeat highly unlikely.

As the statistical record shows, the Arab nations have, in the past, been extremely slow to undertake effective mobilization. Yet each war has further incited the Arabs to modernize and improve their military capability. In the aftermath of each war they have acquired more effective equipment and enhanced their ability to deploy more men in battle; their officers have gained experience and education; and they have been stimulated to make major improvements in their command structure and training methods. Although for some time the Arab nations will remain weak in the air, superior numbers, a modicum of air protection and a Soviet-style artillery force should permit them to fight effectively.

Confronted with such a prospect, Israel—and America—should forthrightly acknowledge some unpleasant facts. Not only are there finite limits to Israel's manpower reserves but Israel is losing population through net emigration—and its emigration statistics include large numbers of better-educated young men of military age who are leaving precisely to avoid the onerous burden of annual military service.[102] Israel's Ministry of Labor and Social Welfare, which does not count most expatriates as permanent departures, still reports that 510,528 Israelis left Israel between 1969 and 1979 as compared with only 384,000 immigrants. Nor is the Soviet Union any longer a substantial source of replenishment, for the number of Soviet Jews emigrating but not settling in Israel has risen from 4.3% in 1973 to 85% in 1981. Thus, as Anthony H. Cordesman, the respected military analyst and Middle East expert, concludes after analyzing the relevant statistics: "Israel does seem to be approaching the absolute limit of its manpower resources, and its manpower may decline in educational quality even if more Israelis do not emigrate."[103]

Thus, if the trend toward polarization continues and the Soviets and other nations increase, or even maintain, their current levels of arms sales and training assistance, Israel's Arab neighbors may soon, even without Egypt, be able to commit, and maintain in combat, reasonably well-trained forces in numbers equalling or surpassing the maximum levels achievable from Israel's limited manpower reservoir.

No doubt Israel will retain a qualitative advantage and the IDF's officers will presumably continue to outclass their Arab opposite numbers, in tactics and strategy. That does not mean, however, that better weapons can, by themselves, always compensate for superior numbers. Training may be even more critical than weapons, for it has been often demonstrated that well-trained personnel can overcome better equipped smaller forces. Since, as has been pointed out, Israel is today losing many of its better educated young people who are seeking careers elsewhere, one may expect some diminution in quality of personnel just at a time when the Arabs are beginning to learn the effective use of the weapon systems they are acquiring. Arab generalship is improving and Arab armies do not have to destroy Israel's cities in order to put the nation in jeopardy; they need only involve the IDF in a protracted war of attrition that would force Israel to remain fully mobilized and exploit the Arab advantage of number.

It is generally accepted doctrine that an offensive force requires at least a 3:1 ratio of advantage to break through a defensive position and if an Arab neighbor, such as Syria, could keep enough of its fighter planes in the air to prevent the IDF from achieving total command of the air, it should be able to deny Israel a quick victory. In that case, the greater manpower and financial resources of the Arab nations might promise them a good chance of ultimate success—a conclusion reinforced by Israel's unexpectedly costly battle with the unprepared Syrians in the course of the Lebanese invasion (see postscript).

Israel's small population sharply limits its ability to fight a protracted war. Nor could its fragile economy long survive the absence of its citizen army. Within months, if not weeks, not only would its economic life grind to a halt but that development could be hastened were the West Bank Palestinians, who supply a large part of Israel's menial labor force, to engage in strikes at a time when Israel's security forces were least able to suppress them.

Need for American Intervention

Sometime before that point the Israeli government would have no option but to call on America to provide not merely money and supplies but military forces. That would create a new and disturbing predicament for both countries.

How would the United States respond? Although our country has no formal security pact with Israel, as it has, for example, with the NATO countries, a succession of America's Presidents and innumerable other political leaders, have repeatedly proclaimed our country's intention to protect the security of Israel. They have found it easy to make that commitment, for few, if any, have seriously considered its implications. Instead they have assumed, without critical thought, that so long as the United States continued to provide ample quantities of weapons and financial aid, Israel could always—as it has done so far—repel military threats with its own armed forces. Indeed, Israeli politicans have ritually proclaimed that Israel has never asked for direct American intervention nor will it ever do so.

Yet even resupply would no longer be easy. At the time of the Yom Kippur War, Portugal was the only NATO nation willing to allow American planes to land at its bases on their way to Israel—and that was because it was then dependent on American arms for its colonial wars. Our other allies denied us landing rights for that purpose. Today, even the government of Portugal could be expected to refuse such rights, leaving the United States with no easy way to get supplies to Israel except by ship. If, due to the lack of refueling bases, resupply had to be undertaken by sea, it would require a minimum of two to three weeks to assemble and load the ships and sail them across the Atlantic and through the Mediterranean.

In the aftermath of the Yom Kippur War many Israelis expressed dark concern that Israel would long be able to defend itself without outside help, but those doubts were resolved by the neutralization of Egypt achieved at Camp David. Yet, even though Israel now has massive stockpiles of supplies and an impressive munitions industry of its own, the realities of Lebanon have once again revived the question. Many Israelis and Israel's American supporters are tacitly acknowledging that the manpower of the IDF alone may not be adequate to assure Israel's defense no matter how much economic and military aid America provides. Thus they are mounting increasing pressure for a formal alliance that would commit America irrevocably to defend Israel within its present extended boundaries.

Israel has already made substantial progress toward securing such a commitment with the Strategic Cooperation Agreement as a first step. Its implications are just now beginning to become apparent as ongoing negotiations translate into hard substance the sketchy and nebulous principles announced last November. Silence has until recently surrounded those discussions, quite likely because the Reagan Administration thought it unwise to reveal the new arrangements so soon after discarding plans for a Jordanian rapid deployment force. In addition, it presumably wished to avoid stimulating Arab opposition too far in advance of the November election. But the Administration is now beginning, bit by bit, to leak the contents of the new agreement. Among other items so far revealed, America is agreeing not only to help Israel develop the Lavi fighter plane, as already announced, but, in addition, a new Israeli missile boat, the Saar-V, while the United States will also conduct a large joint military medical exercise with Israel. More details of the new agreement will undoubtedly be revealed in time for the Administration to gain kudos from Jewish voters in advance of the American elections in November.

During the Carter Administration, when the Pentagon was endeavoring to create a Rapid Deployment Force, the Arab States of the Gulf expressed deep concern at the establishment of an American military presence in the area, and insisted on firm commitments that no American troops deployed there would ever be used to protect Israel against Arab attack but only to repel a Soviet threat or assist the local government in putting down an internal revolt. Today any formal alliance with Israel would, in Arab eyes, mean a dropping of the veil—an irrevocable step toward identifying the United States with the Arabs' enemy, Israel.[104] Those developments cannot help but add momentum to the forces of polarization. The Arabs are fully aware that America's expanded commitments to Israel are strictly unilateral; the Israelis promise nothing in return. Thus they cannot help but calculate that, once these new arrangements are made public Israel will be fully able to dictate the terms on which America sells even the most innocuous arms to Arab nations.[*]

Yet Israel's effort to deny American arms to its Arab neighbors can be tragically self-defeating. As events are showing it is far more likely to spur Arab militarization than hinder it, especially since the Soviet Union stands ready to sell weapons to Arab nations without strings attached and the oil-producing countries command vast financial resources. Nor will that be the only unhappy consequence of polarization. Once the United States is blocked from supplying arms to Arab governments and can thus no longer control the supply of spare parts and replacements, it will have lost any ability to influence the military actions of those governments, just as the American government is now on the verge of losing even theoretical control over Israel's future military by prepositioning supplies in that country. The consequences of permitting Israel to veto the sale of arms to friendly Arab states have been succinctly stated by a well-known American military analyst:

> The U.S. cannot hope to achieve strategic stability in Saudi Arabia, the other friendly Gulf states, Jordan, and Egypt, in an effort to reduce the "worst case" threat to Israel. The end result will be to destroy the U.S. position in the region and possibly to create a unified Arab opposition to the U.S. and Israel that could ultimately make such "worst case" Arab threat a reality, increasing the probability of renewed Soviet politico-strategic intervention. Such restrictions would also have little effect on the Arab military buildup other than making friendly Arab states buy from other nations (like the USSR).[105]

The Next Step — A Formal Security Pact

With admirable candor the leaders of the Israeli lobby have made no effort to conceal the fact that they regard the Strategic Cooperation Agreement as merely the way station to a formal security alliance with America. Denouncing the Reagan Plan of September 1982 as "tilting toward the Arabs," Mr. Thomas A. Dine, the executive director of the Israeli lobby (AIPAC) has called for mobilizing his organization's formidable resources to "transform the relationship between the United States and Israel" or, in other words ". . . finish building the military and economic alliance" between the two countries.

Yet has anyone carefully considered the full implications of a formal

(*) To show how the wind is blowing, one need only note demands by Senator D'Amato of New York that Saudi Arabia should not be given any Stinger missiles until it agrees to abide by the Camp David Agreements, make peace with Israel and stop subsidizing the PLO and the confrontation states. Such terms, requiring changes in its foreign policy unacceptable to it, would, of course, force Saudi Arabia to decline the weapons — which was the real purpose of the D'Amato proposal.

security guarantee to Israel? So long as Israel rejects any further proposals to trade territory for peace, Israel will remain in conflict with most of the Arab nations. Were America to make a formal alliance with Israel we could find ourselves automatically committed to join the fight if and when a shooting war should again resume. If that is not what we want, let us face the realities.

History has repeatedly demonstrated the problems created when nations with disparate objectives join in an alliance. In 1955 Secretary of State Dulles engineered the creation of the Baghdad Pact as part of his "Northern tier" defense against Soviet expansion into the Middle East and Southeast Asia. Pakistan became a signatory to that Pact not because the Pakistanis greatly feared the Communist powers but because of their obsessive fear and hatred of their neighbor, India. They hoped that, once their country was party to a security arrangement sponsored by America, India would be deterred from attacking or, if India did attack America might come to Pakistan's rescue. But that wishful thought was pre-ordained to create disenchantment. When, after China attacked India in 1962, the United States provided arms and equipment to strengthen the Indian armed forces, the Pakistanis were outraged. That action, as they saw it, violated the spirit of the Baghdad Pact. What, they asked, did the United States mean by arming Pakistan's major enemy after it had induced it to become what Americans referred to as an "ally"?

Feeling deceived, Pakistanis developed an angry resentment of the United States. I personally experienced their wrath when President Kennedy sent me in August 1963 to spend three days with President Ayub Khan in an effort to calm the troubled waters. I was only marginally successful; Pakistan-United States relations still suffer from a brooding sense of disillusion.

Nor is that the only example of the mischief implicit in an alliance between parties with contradictory objectives. Portugal experienced much the same sense of betrayal and outrage when, in December 1962, the United States and other NATO powers did nothing to block India's seizure of Goa. Since, under Portugese law, Goa was juridically a part of Portugal, it was, so the Portugese claimed, covered by the protection of the North Atlantic Treaty.

In the light of these incidents, one can easily predict the confusion almost certain to arise from the differing interpretations that would be placed on a formal mutual security pact with Israel—and the damage that might result. Just as the Pakistanis are obsessed with fear of India, Israel is obsessed with fear of its Arab neighbors, and that is its compelling motive for seeking an alliance with America. Such an alliance, in the Israeli's view, is not needed for defense against the Soviets; Israel foresees no immediate threat from Russia and, in any event, the Israelis know that America would automatically respond to any aggressivie Soviet action. What they want is for the United States to help them fight off—or better yet frighten off—their Arab neighbors.

Since that is Israel's objective in seeking an American defense commitment, the Arab nations would instinctively react by applying the old adage that the friend of my enemy is my enemy. As a result, were our country to force the process of polarization to its ultimate fulfillment by formally allying itself with Israel prior to the settlement of its dispute with its Arab neighbors, the United States would be left to defend four million Israelis, fiercely clinging to the territorial profits of past wars, against a minimum of 32 million Arabs who are marching slowly but relentlessly toward modernization and moving with even greater determination toward vastly improved military competence and mobilization.

One need not be a Hegel to recognize that, under these circumstances, an American action that formally aligned out country with Israel would produce an equal and opposite reaction on the Arab side. Instead of discouraging Soviet intervention in the Middle East—which is the Reagan's Administration's stated objectives—such an alliance would encourage and facilitate the spread of Soviet influence, as Russia replaced America as a supplier of Arab arms and a protector of Arab interests. Nor are the Soviets likely to lose interest in the area; indeed, as oil production peaks in the Alaskan, Caucasian and North Sea fields sometime after the year 2000, the oil reservoirs of the Middle East will almost certainly grow in importance not only for Western nations but for Moscow.

Thus there is a very real danger that we might, by concluding a security pact with Israel, set in train a succession of diplomatic moves that would recast the Middle East in a pattern resembling that of the Balkans in 1914. Once America were allied with Israel against the Arab world, an increasing number of Arab states would feel obliged to seek security commitments from the Soviet Union. President Assad has already obtained a Soviet pledge to intervene with force in the event of an Israeli attack against Syria proper (as distinguished from Syrian forces in Lebanon) and the total polarization resulting from an American commitment to Israel could well bring on a superpower clash that neither Moscow nor Washington wished. Just as the great powers lost control in 1914 following the assassination of the Archduke Ferdinand, when the Kaiser gave Austro-Hungary his famous "blank check" while Russia aligned itself on the side of Serbia, so an American blank check to Israel in the form of a security pact that triggered Soviet commitments to the Arab states could leave the involvement of the superpowers to the unpredictable vagaries of Middle East governments. God knows what might then happen! Our country has shown no will to constrain Israeli government actions nor have the Soviets exhibited much ability to control the fiercely nationalistic Syrians.

How could anyone look with equanimity at a war that arrayed America on Israel's side against even a partially mobilized Arab world? Although Secretary of State Haig's concept of a strategic consensus of Middle East nations against Soviet power was demonstrably misbegotten, there is no doubt that turning the Arab world against America would significantly affect the East-West balance. We could expect little, if any, support, or even sympathy, from other Western powers; on the contrary, out of anxiety for a continuance of their oil supplies, some might even be tempted to help the Arab side.

If American intervention under a mutual security pact could lead us into a conflict with cataclysmic overtones, there is another scenario even more disturbing. If Israel were hardpressed by advancing Arab armies and the United States failed to respond to its call for intervention, one cannot rule out the possibility that the Israelis, influenced by the Masada complex they are constantly mentioning, would use—or at least threaten to use—the nuclear weapons they have been building for more than two decades. What then might occur? Would the Arab nations be able to mount a counter-threat with overtones of a *jihad* using nuclear weapons from Pakistan, an Islamic nation closely associated with Jordan? Or would the Soviets respond by providing nuclear arms to the Arabs? They are reported to have promised the Arab nations in 1974 that they would supply such weapons were it to become clear that Israel possessed nuclear arms of its own.[106]

An even more likely reaction might be a Soviet ultimatum—particularly in view of Soviet commitments to Syria—that any Israeli nuclear attack would be countered by Soviet nuclear retaliation against Israel and its total annihilation.

It is hard for me to carry such a grim scenario beyond this point for I do not know how any American government—or the American public—would respond. It is enough to point out that that is the way major wars get started. In this nuclear age we cannot risk another one.

Are Americans Prepared to Fight for Israel?

If an American-Israeli security pact would pose risks of a major war it could also work havoc on the home front. The Vietnam war sharply engraved one lesson on the consciousness of most Americans: never again should we send our young men to fight and die for a cause that the majority of our countrymen do not enthusiastically support. Let us apply that test to Israel.

Political gasconading can be self-deceiving. It is easy for our political leaders to make stirring speeches about their undying fidelity to Israeli security, but America has never had to test its willingness to send troops to defend a beleaguered Israel.[*] No doubt the immediate circumstances surrounding any call for help would play a part in conditioning the reaction, but, whatever the circumstances, the dispatch of young Americans to fight and die for an Israel still holding its conquered territories and at odds with its Arab neighbors might well trigger the most angry and vicious debate since the Civil War. It could create deep and ugly divisions; and, in particular, it might greatly inflame the already ominous antagonisms between Jews and blacks. America's black community is already sensitive to the inequality involved in providing more than its share of our country's military manpower, and no one can foresee the full divisive consequences were America to call on its black soldiers to fight for Israel. The only certainty is that it would stir slumbering resentments and provide a field day for demagogues.

20

Will America Continue Indefinitely to Subsidize Israel's Policies?

IF THE ISRAELI GOVERNMENT CONTINUES to invite the hostility of its Arab neighbors on the untested belief that the United States will come riding to its rescue, it also manages its economic affairs on the assumption, again untested, that America will always be ready with an unlimited checkbook. That assumption needs challenging.

It is difficult to overstate the catastrophic state of the Israeli economy; nor is there any possibility that, so long as Israel persists in rejecting efforts to trade territory for peace, it will ever be able to staunch the drain of resources required to maintain its role as a garrison state with colonialist burdens.

One can measure the degree of decline of the Israeli economy by comparing the histories of the Israeli pound and the Jordanian dinar. In 1948 both of those currencies traded at par with the British pound

(*) A Roper poll in February 1981 showed that only 26% of Americans would favor sending U.S. troops if Arab forces invaded Israel, while 58% opposed such an action and 16% had no opinion. Cited in Curtis, *A Changing Image*, p. 206.

which was then worth $2.80. Since then the Jordanian dinar has declined only slightly to a value of $2.68, while the Israeli pound has deteriorated to the point where it is now worth 1/40 of a cent.[107] Israel's foreign debt now exceeds $29 billion — or over $7000 per capita — and is rising rapidly. One can appreciate its magnitude by comparing it to the current Argentine foreign debt of $44 billion which hangs like a menacing cloud over the international banking community, even though, for a country of 30 million people, it amounts to only $1500 per capita. The critical difference is that in countries such as Mexico, Argentina and Brazil the proportion of the debt owing foreign banks is in the 65% to 80% range, whereas the largest part of Israel's foreign debt consists of long-term obligations of the government of Israel on concessionary terms. Well over $9 billion is owed to the United States government while more than $3 billion reflects the sale of "Israel bonds" largely to the United States Jewish community. Another major component of the debt ($6.5 billion at the end of 1982) consists of external resident deposits mobilized through the Israeli banking system, which are classified as short term credit to the Israeli economy.

In its relations with the United States, Israel recalls President Reagan's favorite fantasy of the "welfare queen" who drives a Rolls Royce. Although the Israeli standard of living is not high by Western standards (approximately $6600 per capita) it increased by approximately 20% from 1978 to 1982 while productivity rose only 4% during that same period. Israel's economic health is directly affected by its territorial expansion; ever since 1967, when it first imposed its military occupation on conquered Arab lands and people, its economy has steadily declined while America's subsidy has steadily risen — and those curves are diverging at an accelerating pace. Israel's invasion of Lebanon is estimated to have cost $3 billion while its continued occupation of Lebanon is reputedly costing $1 million a day. Meanwhile, Israel is suffering a massive balance of payments deficit, and an inflation rate of more than 400% a year.[108]

ISRAELI INFLATION AVERAGE

Years	Cumulative Rate of Change	Annual Increase
1960-67	47.4%	5.9%
1968-73	55.6	9.3
1974-78	195.5	33.3
1979-84(*)	1,200.0	200.0

(*) Estimate

If our subsidy is unhealthy for the recipient it is increasingly irksome for the donor. Although in the past much of our military aid has been extended on a loan basis, the Congress is now providing all our aid to Israel as a grant—which means that this year the American taxpayers are *giving* Israel more than $2.6 billion. Much of Israel's debt to the United States of $9 billion reflects "soft" loans with long terms and interest rates far below the normal market; still, Israel's supporters are now assiduously preparing a drive to secure the forgiveness of those debts and they seem likely to succeed. Once our government begins forgiving Israel's huge debt, American taxpayers will be required to contribute at an ever higher rate in years ahead.

Today the American government is considering proposals to put Israeli aid on a multi-year basis so that it will not be vulnerable to the need for annual appropriations. At the same time the Israeli Treasury is reported in *The Jerusalem Post* (International Edition), August 12-18, 1984 to be preparing an aid request for next year amounting to $5 billion.

Such a level of aid is approaching the ridiculous. To hand out $5 billion next year to Israel would mean to give a country with a population only slightly larger than that of metropolitan Washington, DC, almost one-third of the total United States foreign and economic assistance we provide the two to three billion people in the Third World.

The comparison most startling for Americans, however, is that the level of aid proposed by Israel would mean a handout of American taxpayers' money to a tiny country in an amount equal to one-third of the budget of the Housing and Urban Development Department (HUD), which is a major instrument of help for low-income Americans. Or to take another comparison, it is a sum one-fourth bigger than the total budget of the United States Environmental Protection Agency (EPA) and 1250 times the size of the budget of the Small Business Administration (SBA).

At a time when the United States is harassed by crushing budget deficits, such disproportionate largesse for Israel would seem to have no chance of approval; yet the Administration and the Congress are likely to settle on a sum approaching that magnitude. In that event, it should be carefully explained to the American people that their taxes are being used to provide Israel with an annual sum roughly equal to $1500 for every Israeli man, woman and child; or $7500 for each Israeli family of five.

Meanwhile, thoughtful Israelis, such Rafael Benvenisti, the economist who heads the government's Investment Authority, points out that the "American connection" has discouraged the Israeli government from coming to grips with its current economic catastrophe. In *The Christian Science Monitor* of August 21, 1984, he is quoted as saying "There is always the belief, among the public and politicians, that no matter how bad things get, somebody—basically the US—will come to our aid. The idea is 'If you have the bank behind you, who cares?'" Benvenisti's comments, which reflect the views of many in Israel, confirm the thesis that the excessive zeal of American politicians to demonstrate allegiance to Israel is contributing to Israel's financial delinquencies as well as to the paralysis of its search for peace. It is a lesson the American Jewish community should ponder carefully; after all, overindulgence to a dependent can be a cruel disservice whether that dependent be a child or a small nation.

If Israel's government were convincingly seeking peace—if it were offering to make concessions as well as exact privileges—the American people might for a long while continue—as they are now doing—to let their tax money be used to pay half of Israel's military budget and provide massive economic aid in addition. But no Likud Government is likely to show such a change of heart, and the action of an Alignment government or a grand coalition remains untested.

The fact that the Congress has continued year after year to increase our subsidy without regard to America's own budget stringencies or the state of the American economy is one of the more remarkable phenomena of American politics. It testifies not merely to the strength of the Israeli lobby but to the underlying political power of the American Jewish Community. That power should not be denigrated; it is the result of the exceptional political awareness and dedication of American Jews which they by no means restrict to relations with Israel. Unlike all too many of our countrymen, America's Jewish population is not politically indifferent or apathetic; as befits good citizens, American Jews are politically *engagé*. They are the most selfless promoters of causes; and, in political as in other matters, they are extraordinarily generous both with their time and their money.

Yet the degree of the Israeli lobby's hold over Congress is excessive and unhealthy, as was decribed by Robert G. Kaiser in "The U.S. Risks Suffocating Israel With Kindness", *The Washington Post*, May 27, 1984:

> Earlier, the House and Senate engaged in a bit of a contest over who would give more to the Israelis this year. The Reagan administration requested $850 million in economic (as opposed to military) aid for the next year. The Senate Foreign Relations Committee—whose chairman and ranking Democrat are both up for re-election this November, as one of their colleagues noted—quickly upped the ante to $1.2 billion, an increase of nearly 50 percent. This worried members of the House Foreign Affairs Committee, according to one senior member. "We can't let them be more generous to Israel than we are," he quoted colleagues as saying. In the end, the House committee proposed $1.1 billion, "but it will come out of conference at $1.2 billion," a knowledgeable member predicted.

Episodes like these get no serious coverage in the news media. In Washington, reporters and politicans share a cynical understanding that Israel and its American friends constitute probably the single most effective lobbying force in the country; they take its victories for granted.

Ask a senator or congressman on one of the committees involved if anyone this year seriously questioned whether the huge amount of American aid to Israel was a good idea, and you are more likely to get a laugh than an answer.

No one can predict with precision how long Israel's supporters will be able to wield the overpowering clout this incident suggests, but one can expect counter pressures to begin to build sooner or later. The aid now expected from America is disproportionate to the point of absurdity, and if the Israeli lobby pushes its luck beyond a certain undefinable point, its exactions will trigger a revolt. Sooner or later some demagogue will be tempted to capitalize on prejudice and ethnic enmities and the grimier subsurface rancor of American society. One need not be a profound student of politics to be aware of the rapid cyclical swings in opinion that characterize our system or to predict that Americans will not indefinitely continue each year doling out funds for uses that appear to undercut our national interests.

Thus, Israel's American supporters would be well advised to inform Jerusalem that the current state of affairs is illusory, a transient aberration of domestic politics, and that, unless Israel pursues policies more in line with America's interests in the Middle East, our huge annual outlay of gifts and soft loans may, at some point, be abruptly curtailed.

In addition, if they do not improve their manners Israel's leaders can, by arrogance that borders on contempt, contribute to the rebellion that seems likely to occur. Comments that patronize America—and there have been many during the Likud period—are nourishing resentments under the surface. At the same time the current alarm over mounting international debts could play a critical role. If Israel were to seek the forgiveness of its huge $9 billion debt to the United States government without taking any of the austerity measures imposed by the IMF on other financially distressed nations and if Israeli leaders continue to insist—as many presumptuously do—that America owes Israel for its efforts against Lebanon and the PLO, it will disenchant an increasing number of Americans.

Israel's Recent Elections

Although it is impossible to predict with precision just when a reaction against our aid to Israel may occur or what form it may take, the timing and intensity are likely to be influenced—at least to some extent—by the vagaries of Israel's domestic politics. During the period of soul-searching and discontent that followed the failure of Israel's Lebanese escapade many, both in Israel and America, awaited Israel's July elections with mixed hope and apprehension. Were the Labor Alignment to obtain a decisive majority, they saw at least a chance that the search for a peace settlement might be renewed with serious intent, even though it was far from clear that a Labor government would have the vision, will, political courage, and flexibility essential for even the beginning of negotiations; they remembered that it was, after all, a Labor government that first devised the stratagem of "creating new facts" through the construction of West Bank settlements.

But, if progress toward peace could not be assured even though the Labor Alignment were to win a large majority, there could be no doubt whatever that an impressive victory for a Likud-led coalition would guarantee a continued state of dangerous confrontation. Moreover, it seemed probable that, were the Likud to be returned to power, the "oriental jews" (largely immigrants from the North African Maghreb who are now a numerical majority) would move toward political dominance. In that event the result of the election might roughly parallel that of the 1948 election in South Africa which installed the Afrikaaners in permanent control of the government and institutionalized apartheid as a metastasizing cancer in the body politic.

As events turned out, Israel's ambiguous decision at the polls settled nothing; indeed it did little but dramatize the extent to which the Lebanese misadventure had contributed to the nation's political fragmentation. As it appears at the time this is written (early August 1984) the inevitable consequence of the stalemated vote is an indefinite period of political paralysis during which Israel will be disabled from taking any positive steps toward achieving peace with its neighbors. Although some compromise measures are imperative to alleviate the appalling financial and economic condition of the country, the imposition of the austerity measures required to restore even a limited measure of viability to Israel's battered economy could trigger political repercussions and the further intensification of factional discontent. To be sure, both parties are under heavy pressure to commence a phased withdrawal of some units of the IDF from southern Lebanon, and that may well be undertaken. But the settlements program is unlikely to be stopped (although it may be slowed for financial reasons) nor is there any realistic chance that the opposing political factions can overcome strong forces of inertia and *immobilisme* and once again crank up the now badly-rusted peace machinery.

Had they the will to do so, Israel's American supporters could no doubt give a significant impetus to the renewal of peace efforts. But, institutionally musclebound, they seem destined to continue that indiscriminate applause and encouragement which validate the lowest common denominator of Israeli politics. Thus there seems little chance that they will use their inherently formidable influence to encourage new initiatives for peace or even to arrest the dangerous process of polarization now in progress.

American Jewish Organizations

In writing frankly about the current situation I do not mean to imply that the objective of polarization reflects the conscious and informed wish of most American Jews. In fact, many of my Jewish friends are as worried as I that the lobby's heavyhanded pressure on Congress and the Executive to strengthen Israel and weaken its neighbors will contribute to polarization—a concern that is strongly and publicly ventilated by thoughtful friends in Israel. But the institutional arrangements for expressing American Jewish support for Israel through money, propaganda and political action frustrate efforts to slow or redirect a process that has now acquired a dynamic of its own.

The problem is well illustrated by the comment of Mr. Kenneth Bialkin, the new chairman of the Conference of Major American Jewish Organizations who has now become a principal spokesman for the American Jewish community. Speaking just before the recent Israel elections Mr. Bialkin was quoted in *The Jerusalem Post* (International Edition), July 8-14, 1984, as stating: "If the Alignment wins and changes Israel's policies, we will support them; if the Likud wins and pursues a strong line in the West Bank we will get behind them."

Although Mr. Bialkin was unconsciously paraphrasing Stephen Decatur's theme of "my country right or wrong", there is a significant difference. Stephen Decatur was speaking of his own country, the United States, not of a friendly foreign state. Mr. Bialkin seems quite indifferent to the fact that Israel's pursuit of "a strong line in the West Bank" would contravene an expressed objective of American policy.

I can only conclude that Marshall McLuhan was wrong in asserting that the medium is the message; in today's overorganized world the institution is all too often the message, and the institutions created to support Israel put excruciating pressure on America's Jewish citizens to prove to their peers—by financial and political support—that they have a Stephen Decatur commitment toward that country. Admittedly, a brief cessation of uncritical applause occurred following the Sabra and Shatilla massacres. Most American Jews then suffered deep anguish and even leaders of some Jewish organizations expressed their torment in public, but following the Kahan Commission Report, apologias once more began to appear.

21

The Need for a Middle East Policy to Serve American Interests

I MENTIONED EARLIER that the Lebanese invasion should teach us two lessons—one of general application and one specifically related to the Middle East. The Middle East lesson—and it is urgent—is that America must devise and pursue a policy tailored to its own interests, which are many and complex. We can no longer be content merely to react to policies made in Jerusalem nor can we any longer afford to play the role of Israel's overly-indulgent guardian, uncomplainingly paying larger and larger bills and dutifully sweeping up the breakage produced by the ambitions of Israel's leaders. We are a great country and we should act like one.

That means that we should systematically recast our relations with Israel, since, as presently conceived, they are unhealthy for both countries: unhealthy for Israel because our undiscriminating support encourages the most reckless zealots of Israeli expansionism; unhealthy for the United States because, if we continue as a silent accessory to Israel's hegemonic fantasies, we shall destroy what is left of our prestige and authority in the Middle East. What is more—as our Lebanese ordeal should have warned us—playing the role of Israel's obedient spear-bearer could someday involve us in conflicts that could lead to a dangerous East-West clash.

But to recast our relations with Israel we must first sweep away the inhibitions that preclude Americans from discussing Middle East policy cooly and rationally; only then can we fashion our relations with Israel as we fashion our relations with other friendly countries, by seeking to determine what best serves the interests of both parties and, at the same time, satisfies international requirements of fairness. Our current relations with Israel do not meet that test. They are too badly skewed to persist for any protracted period; unless we deliberately reshape them they may be violently reshaped by events in a manner harmful to both sides.

Yet I do not wish to be misunderstood. If there are compelling reasons why we should redesign our relations with Israel on a mutually self-respecting basis, there are equally strong reasons why we should continue our concern for Israel's security and keep on supplying reasonable financial and economic help. But we should be quite certain that our security assistance and financial aid are provided within the framework of a relationship that reflects the interests of both sides.

America cannot afford another Lebanese fiasco, yet we will succeed in avoiding such involuntary involvements only if our Executive and Legislative branches enforce America's contract rights and apply America's laws against Israel just as they do against any other nation. They should not be deterred from doing their duty by the vacuous accusation that that would be "putting pressure on Israel", as though that were a sacrilege. America, after all, is a sovereign nation with its own interests to advance and defend.

Israel Lacks the Attributes of an Ally of America

The glib assertion that "Israel is America's most dependable ally in the Middle East" has become so deeply embedded in the boilerplate of political rhetoric as to acquire a false validity. Yet that proposition cannot withstand the most elementary analysis. Even without reference to earlier history, the events recorded on these pages make vividly clear that Israel is not an ally and that our relations lack the basic attributes of an alliance:

(1) the interests and objectives of the two countries are far from congruent;

(2) as a military ally Israel would offer America far greater disadvantages than benefits; and

(3) Israel habitually fails to concert its policies with ours or even consult before taking unilateral actions.

(1) THE UNITED STATES AND ISRAEL DO NOT HAVE CONGRUENT INTERESTS AND OBJECTIVES

The United States is a world power with interests in every part of the globe; its policies in any key area must, therefore, take account of the sensitivities and interests of other friendly nations and be consistent with its larger strategies. Israel is a tiny nation surrounded by hostile neighbors; it is understandably obsessed with its own parochial concerns. Although Israel's American supporters assert, as though it were a message from the mountain top, that what is good for Israel is good for America and that the interests of the two countries are congruent, Israel's leaders know better. As the then Foreign Minister (now Prime Minister) Yitzhak Shamir said at the time of the first abortive discussions of a Strategic Cooperation Agreement on December 15, 1981 "Much as we want to coordinate our activities with the United States, the interests are not identical. We have to, from time to time, worry about our own interests".[109]

The question whether Israel's interests are congruent with America's cannot be answered in the abstract. That Israelis disagree among themselves as to the nature of Israel's true interests is not relevant to the current issue. The question of an alliance does not concern Israel's interests as they might, for example, be identified by members of the Israeli Peace Movement; the relevant point of reference is its interests as defined by past experience and by the leaders who govern Israeli politics.

Members of the Likud coalition—who are certainly powerful enough to block any peace initiative—regard as an essential Israeli objective, the maintenance of Israel's control of its occupied territories, even though that may subject their country to protracted struggle and the burdens of a garrison state. As the Lebanese invasion attested, Israel's Likud faction has opted for hegemony rather than co-existence.

America's interests, on the contrary, are clearly incompatible with that objective. America has no reason to help Israel keep its occupied territories; on the countrary we Americans should regard it as abhorrent to identify our country with Israel's increasingly regressive rule over a million and a half Palestinians and other Arabs. Instead, to be true to our cherished principles, we should—in arms-length discussions and using the full political leverage at our command—try to persuade the Israelis to trade those territories for peace, as they did with the Sinai sand dunes, while at the same time using the depleted leverage remaining to us to try to influence Arab leaders.

America has a practical interest in Persian Gulf oil and a political interest in maintaining friendly relations with 100 million Arabs who, as the winds of change sweep the Middle East, will become an increasingly articulate and politically powerful force in world politics. In the present atmosphere of hostility and violence pervading that turbulent area there is no way one can reconcile an American-Israeli alliance with the maintenance of friendly Arab relations. Security commitments imply an identifiable common enemy or range of enemies, expressed or implied. The Israelis would see little value in an alliance commitment limited to the Soviet threat, while the Arab world would see a United States-Israeli alliance, no matter how the commitments were qualified, as aimed at them. It would, in the view of Arab leaders, make the United States the enemy of all the Arab states.

Supporters of an alliance favor it as guaranteeing the *status quo*, but, from America's point of view, the *status quo* is an unhealthy state of affairs—nor can it long continue. The current frozen stalemate clearly works to erode America's whole stake in the Middle East.(*) Our country is not well served when our constantly increasing handouts enable Israel to live beyond its means on an American dole, and I am amazed that any of Israel's American supporters regard such a condition as indefinitely sustainable. I find it quite unrealistic to ask our country to be more generous to Israel's citizens than to its own needful citizens, and, as the public finally becomes aware of the excessive magnitude of our Israeli subsidy, that massive outlay is likely sooner or later to be abruptly halted in an atmosphere of anger and acrimony.

At the heart of the Arab-Israeli struggle is the failure to find any formula that even minimally satisfies the needs of the Palestinian people for self-determination and a homeland of their own. For seventeen years, the United States tried to resolve that problem through diplomatic means but with only limited success. With the advent of the Reagan Administration, Secretary of State Alexander Haig sought to reinterpret the problem in terms of the superpower rivalry with which he was obsessed; he approached the solution by conditioned reflex almost solely in military terms. He seems naively to have accepted the propaganda thesis that, because Israel has fought mostly successful wars with its Arab neighbors, it can be a bastion of strength in defending the area against a Soviet incursion. But that again is a glib slogan that passes for wisdom only because it escapes rigorous scrutiny.

(2) ISRAEL COULD NOT BE A USEFUL MILITARY ASSET TO AMERICA IN DEFENDING THE MIDDLE EAST

The claim that Israel is a useful ally of the United States has escaped the test of the intellectual marketplace for only one reason. As with other aspects of United States-Israeli relations it has become politically untouchable.

That was made clear beyond the shadow of a doubt eight years ago when the then Chairman of the Joint Chiefs, General George S. Brown, was sufficiently indiscreet as to give an honest answer in an interview with an Israeli cartoonist and contributing editor to *Newsweek International,* named Ranan Lurie. Asked by Mr. Lurie whether "Israel and its forces were more a burden or more a blessing, from a purely military point of view, to the United States," Brown replied:, "I think it's just got to be considered a burden."

(*) "If the peace process fails or drags on too long, as now seems likely, it may act to discredit both the U.S. and the conservative Gulf regimes that have backed peace with Israel. It may force King Hussein to tilt toward the Soviet Union and force Syria into still closer dependence on the Soviets. It may lead to another major war between Israel and Syria and make Lebanon the partitioned 'killing ground' for both states. . . . It may also stimulate Gulf involvement in the almost inevitable next round between the Arabs and Israel. Cordesman, *op., cit.,* pp. 61, 62.

Although that interview occurred on April 12, 1976, it was not published until October 17th, and there was speculation that publication had been deliberately held up to embarrass President Ford just prior to election time. In any event the General's candid professional view provoked outraged cries from Israel's diligent American spokesmen as well as from its friends in Congress, many of whom called for Brown's dismissal. As a result he was subjected to public criticism both by the President and the Secretary of Defense.

In view of the public pillorying that followed Brown's forthright assessment of Israel's military usefulness no member of the Joint Chiefs of Staff or any high ranking officer in the United States Armed Services is likely to utter any similar heresy, since the incident made it clear that the issue was primarily political and not to be subjected to the rigorous tests of professional analysis.

Nevertheless, General Brown's expanded remarks deserve careful consideration. "If the trends were reversed," he said, "then I could see in the long term where (Israel's forces) might be a tremendous asset, where they could gain power and could bring stability in the area." But, he predicted, the Arab's wealth would enable them to "overcome the deficiency that they've had, which is leadership, and technology and educated people." Thus the apparently inevitable growth in Arab power, Brown said, would perhaps necessitate "a complete change in outlook on Israel's part."[110]

As the facts and discussion in this book tend to show, such an analysis is both cogent and prescient, for there is no question that Arab military strength is expanding and will continue to expand while— particularly in Syria with Soviet help and elsewhere with assistance from Western Europe—one can expect a major improvement in Arab military leadership and technology.

The essential point implied, though not made explicit, by General Brown is that Israel cannot be a strategic asset to the United States so long as it remains in a state of hostility with its Arab neighbors. If entered into prior to a peace settlement, a security pact would amount to little more than an American pledge to help Israel maintain its current territorial acquisitions—the Golan Heights, the Gaza Strip, the West Bank and East Jerusalem—and even a still undefined portion of southern Lebanon.

One should not, of course, rule out a possible alliance with Israel once it has made peace with its Arab neighbors; indeed as a part of any final settlement agreement the United States might well guarantee not only Israel's borders but the territorial integrity of all states joining in the settlement. But to talk of Israel as an ally so long as it is completely surrounded by states with which it is formally at war is nonsense. That point has been forcefully made by Andrew H. Cordesman. In dismissing the "strategic relationship" contemplated by the Strategic Cooperation Agreement President Reagan announced in November 1983, Cordesman writes:

> Such a strategic relationship is militarily purposeless and hopelessly unstable without an Arab-Israeli peace, and any U.S. use of Israel as a base for USCENTCOM forces would do the West far more harm than good. The end result of any U.S. use of Israel to deal with a contingency in any Arab state would be to destroy the legitimacy of all Arab regimes friendly to the U.S. and to kill any U.S. hope of strategic partnership with the Gulf states. Similarly, such a relationship does not provide a convincing U.S. security guarantee to Israel by joint naval and air force exercises or by prestocking equipment in Israel. The net effect of such policies will be to isolate the U.S., weaken moderate Arab states, and increase the threat to Israel.
>
> Although it may be some time before the opportunity arises, the U.S. should focus on trading economic and military assistance to Israel for Israel's support of peace and not for "surrogate" forces.[111]

Even when the issue addressed by General Brown is considered in its larger politico-military context, the opinion he expressed is eminently correct for a number of reasons:

FIRST, the United States cannot cooperate militarily with Israel without irreparably damaging its relations with the Arab states. Having repeatedly observed the United States' uncritical support of Israeli actions, the Arab nations regard such cooperation as a menace to their own security. They have learned from the Lebanese episode, as well as other past experiences that, if arms are made available to Israel, the United States will do nothing to control their use; thus they are confident that if American arms are prepositioned on Israeli soil no matter what formal custodial arrangements are made, the Israelis will use them as they wish—even in the pursuit of hegemonic objectives. If vague talk of United States-Israel military cooperation sends shudders throughout the Arab world, serious consideration of a security pact of the kind the Israeli lobby is now promoting would set the Arab world solidly against America.

SECOND, Israél's physical limitations deny its utility as a significant strategic asset. Israel is too small a country to sustain a United States military base in the context of the Middle Eastern politico-military environment since the fact of an alliance would make it a tiny island in a hostile Arab sea. In addition, Israel's military might depends on a citizen army and its already weak economy would collapse in case of a protracted war. Quite clearly it is Israel, not the United States, that would benefit from an alliance relation. Once that alliance had resulted in complete polarization, Israel would become not an American military asset but a hostage island in a sea of hostile Arab nations which our country could rescue only at enormous political and military costs.

THIRD, there is no way Israeli military power can effectively be deployed beyond its own immediate neighborhood. None of the Arab states that encircle Israel would, no matter how desperate they might be, dare to accept help from the IDF or tolerate Israeli forces on its soil or permit Israeli forces to cross its territory in transit elsewhere. Thus the IDF could not pass through Jordan to attack Syria (as its strategic plans are rumored to contemplate) without having to fight its way. That point was dramatically demonstrated in September 1970 when the Jordanian army was locked in battle with the PLO and Syria was threatening to intervene against it on the PLO side. Although units of the IDF were massed on the truce line to intervene in support of a desperately beleaguered Jordan, King Hussein still ordered his army to repel any Israeli forces crossing the frontier. The Arabs have learned from experience that if Israeli troops move into their country, only armed forces can remove them.

FOURTH, the proposal for a military alliance with Israel misses the central strategic point: the real menace to the Middle East is not external aggression but the political fragility of most of the Arab nations and their vulnerability to subversion and destabilization. For that reason the United States should concentrate on avoiding disruptive quarrels rather than on security commitments or even the stockpiling of military hardware that create resentment and uneasiness, since turmoil provides a fertile soil for the burgeoning of Soviet and other anti-Western influences. Here again—as revealed by the Lebanon adventure—Israel's calculus differs from America's. By using American-provided weapons to attack Syria in 1982 without our advance knowledge, Israel precipitated a major expansion of the Soviet presence and a major increase in Soviet influence in the area—to America's disadvantage.

FIFTH, advocates of an alliance with Israel make much of the contention that Israel provides America with invaluable intelligence information and the results of combat experience in disclosing the weaknesses and capabilities of our advanced weapons. Yet, isn't that the least the Israelis can do? After all, we have given them the weapons and we subsidize their economy. Even so, General Sharon, as Defense Minister, did not hesitate to carry impudence beyond all acceptable limits by shutting off the transfer of such intelligence to show his displeasure with American policy.

Moreover, offsetting any intelligence benefits is the fact that, when, without our knowledge or approval, Israel flew F-15s and F-16s over Iraq in 1982, it seriously risked the compromise of our weapons technology. Then again, when it attacked the Syrian armies in Lebanon, it disclosed to the Syrians and thus to the Russians the exact performance of our smart bombs and other weapons.

FINALLY, to be true to itself, the United States must maintain generally accepted standards of international morality. Yet our country transgresses those standards when it aids and abets the military invasion of Lebanon, condones the Israeli settlements policy which violates the Fourth Geneva Convention, and averts its gaze from Israel's repressive behavior in its occupied territories.

(3) ISRAEL DOES NOT CONSULT OR CONCERT POLICIES WITH AMERICA

If Israel and the United States lack the commonality of interest required of allies, Israel also fails the test of consultation. When the Begin government misrepresented its intentions in invading Lebanon it was only following an established Israeli practice. In launching military operations Israel has again and again either deliberately deceived the United States, as in the case of its Suez attack in 1956 and its drive to Beirut in 1982, or has acted without advance notice, as when it attacked Iraq's nuclear reactor in 1981. It has repeatedly used American-supplied equipment in violation of the restrictions to which it had agreed.

Need for a New Self-Respecting Relationship

If Israel is not an ally of the United States, how should we refashion our relations? Clearly the United States has a special interest in Israel's welfare since Israel is, for many Jewish Americans, not a foreign nation so much as the expression of ethnic memory and religious obligation, a badge of legitimacy, a reparation for the anguished millenia of the Diaspora, a consolation for the Holocaust and a symbol of the strength and unity required to prevent its repetition. Most Americans—and I include myself—sympathize with this view. We want a close relationship with Israel that is good for both sides and consistent with America's other interests and objectives.

If, as I have sought to show, the present distorted relationship is not good for America, is it still good for Israel? To answer that question we should reexamine a second assumption on which our policy has been based—the assumption that, by arming Israel to the point where it is militarily superior to any combination of states in the area, the Israelis will overcome their defensive neuroses and strive for peaceful relations with their Arab neighbors.

That assumption, as I have earlier shown, has been sadly disproven by experience. In our anxiety to build up Israel's sense of security we have helped turn it into an expansionist nation, intolerant of its neighbors, while its current government no longer accepts the thesis of Resolution 242 of the United Nations Security Council that it should exchange conquered territory for peace.

As a result of our excessively indulgent military aid, we have encouraged Israel to build a military establishment that consumes nearly 50% of its national budget and imposes an enormous burden on its economy, thus leaving it increasingly dependent on our ever-mounting economic largesse. At the same time, by providing our aid without inspection and overlooking Israel's disregard for the restrictions we place on its use, we encourage its use for expansionist objectives that can, in the long run, destroy Israel.

I do not see how anyone can view Israel's future with optimism so long as it continues to pursue its current policy lines. The hegemonic designs revealed by its Lebanese adventure not only negate Israel's original promise but deny its future. So long as there is no peace in the Middle East but only a protracted period of non-war punctuated by armed combat, time will continue to work against Israel. For, as we have seen from the Lebanese experience, Israel emerges from new wars relatively less strong than before, since conflict leads to fear and fear goads even the most lethargic Arab states to greater military preparations.

The Arabs moreover think in long time spans. Israel has been in existence only 40 years but the crusaders were in the Middle East for 200 years. Where are they now?

Up to this point Israel has capitalized heavily on two assets: the American cornucopia and Arab lethargy and disunity. But it cannot count indefinitely on such assets so long as it continues to prefer territory to peace. If, as I believe, we have overarmed Israel and encouraged it to pursue self-destructive ambitions, we have insufficiently armed and equipped it for the continued pursuit of those ambitions, since sooner or later Israel's expansionism may compel the Arabs to achieve that unity of action it most greatly fears.

That is the ultimate lesson of Lebanon.

22

The Errors and Betrayals—
A Recapitulation

Errors by the United States

1. Our government erred in not making clear from the outset that it strongly opposed Israel's invasion of Lebanon; instead it uttered only feeble cautions which the Israelis interpreted as a green light.

2. Our government erred when it failed to impose on Israel the sanctions provided by American law for misusing equipment supplied it exclusively for self-defense—first, to commit an unprovoked attack (a clear *casus belli*) on Iraq's OSIRAK reactor in 1981, and second, to invade Lebanon and attack Syria in violation of the United Nations Charter.

3. Our government erred when, after voting for a United Nations Security Council resolution calling on Israel to stop its aggression and return unconditionally to its own borders, it vetoed any sanctions to enforce that resolution, then compounded its hypocrisy by doing nothing to deter Israel from using its American-supplied weapons to bomb and shoot its way clear to Beirut.

4. Our government erred once again when, having voted for a Security Council Resolution on August 1, 1982, "demanding" an immediate cease-fire and the dispatch of UN observers to make sure it was maintained, it failed to react when Israel scornfully rejected the Resolution and continued to destroy large parts of West Beirut with American-supplied weapons.

5. Our government erred when it failed to overrule Israel's objections to a UN peacekeeping force to separate the warring factions during the PLO withdrawal; it erred even more when it committed our Marines as part of a multi-national force in an environment rife with violence and anti-American sentiment.

6. Our goverment erred when—despite Israel's long record of broken promises—it relied on Israel's commitment to persuade the PLO leaders to leave Lebanon by promising that the United States would "do its utmost" to safeguard the Palestinians remaining behind. Instead of doing its utmost, our government did nothing. Prematurely withdrawing our marines, we left hundreds of Palestinian men, women, and children to be massacred in the Sabra and Shatilla camps.

7. Our government erred when it muttered only feeble protests for five weeks while the IDF used the equipment we had supplied to blow to pieces West Beirut and many of its inhabitants. We did not seriously threaten—much less apply—the sanctions provided by our laws.

8. Our government erred when

    (a) it sat silent while the Israeli government bullied our country by arrogantly threatening "that Israel was losing its patience" and would invade West Beirut unless our diplomats hurried faster to conclude an agreement for expelling the PLO leaders; and it erred again when it condoned

    (b) the continued rain of shells and bombs on West Beirut even after the PLO withdrawal agreement had been largely concluded, thus seriously jeopardizing our negotiations.

9. Our government erred when it uttered only a mild rebuke after Israel broke its agreement to the cease-fire arrangements on September 15, 1982, by occupying West Beirut, then took no action when Israel rejected our request to return to the agreed lines.

10. Our government erred when it permitted Israel, even after the Sabra and Shatilla massacres, to brush aside our request that its forces return to the cease-fire lines; instead the IDF held its advanced position for ten more days until outraged world opinion finally forced Israel's hand.

11. Our government erred when it did not insist that Israel halt its settlements program but continued to subsidize that program even after President Reagan strongly urged the "immediate adoption of a settlement freeze" on the ground that such a freeze was indispensable to the creation of confidence needed for "wider participation" in the peace talks.

12. Our government erred in uncritically believing the Israeli assumption that the Gemayel government could gain effective control of the whole of Lebanon.

13. Our government erred in changing the mission of our marines from peace-keeping to active support of the minority regime in a civil war that was none of our business.

14. Our government erred in negotiating the May 17 agreement, which, by giving Israel a presence in southern Lebanon, assured the resistance and antagonism of the Shiites who live in that area.

15. Our government erred when it disregarded elementary diplomatic practice by negotiating to obtain concessions for Israel that seriously compromised Lebanese sovereignty without simultaneously discussing with Syria the terms of its own withdrawal; thus offending Assad by confronting him with a *fait accompli.*

16. Our government erred when it continued to maintain our marines at the Beirut airport after the IDF had made clear its intention to withdraw from the Chouf Mountains, since that withdrawal would inevitably expose our troops to cross-fire.

17. Our government erred in closely associating itself with a minority Gemayel government and not making our support of that government explicitly contingent on Gemayel's broadening its base through concessions to the other ethnic and religious factions.

18. Our government erred when it continued to try to establish the Gemayel regime as a central government with its authority extending throughout the country even after Israel had given up the enterprise as hopeless and withdrawn to south Lebanon.

19. Our government erred when it continued to insist that the Gemayel government ratify the May 17 agreement in spite of the fact that its adherence to that agreement precluded it from enlarging its base to include other factions essential to its survival.

20. Our government erred in naively accepting the Israeli view that Lebanon could be united and restored to quiet merely by destroying the PLO armed forces and driving out the PLO leaders. Even more fundamental, our government failed to recognize that Israel's main objective in seeking to destroy the PLO as a political force was to render the West Bank Palestinians leaderless so it could impose its will without interference.

21. Our government erred in continuing an unwise and unseemly self-denying ordinance not to talk or negotiate with the PLO, the only representatives recognized by the Palestinians.

22. Our government erred in insisting that the Palestinians must be represented by Jordan and denying them the right of self-determination, even though the West Bank Palestinians have no wish to return to Jordanian rule, nor could. Jordan incorporate almost 800,000 Palestinians without serious destablizing effects.

23. Our government erred in joining Israel in a Strategic Cooperation Agreement that had the effect

(a) of disqualifying our marines from playing a neutral peacekeeping role at a time when they were still committed to such a mission;

(b) of seriously impairing America's ability to play a mediating role in the Middle East by further alienating key Arab states;

(c) of impairing America's ability to influence Arab nations to exercise restraint toward Israel;

(d) of diminishing our control over Israeli actions in the event of another war by providing for the pre-positioning of supplies in Israel;

(e) of driving Arab states toward other arms suppliers, and primarily the Soviet Union.

24. Our government erred when it persistently failed to call the Israeli government to account for its long series of deceptions and misrepresentations.

Betrayals by Israel

1. Israel betrayed the United States when Prime Minister Begin falsely assured President Reagan on January 9, 1982, that Israel would not invade Lebanon without clear provocation, then fabricated a transparently contrived provocation and invaded on June 6, 1982.

2. Israel broke its word to us when Prime Minister Begin gave a written assurance to President Reagan that, in invading Lebanon, the IDF would go only 25 miles north of the boundary, and then sent the IDF shooting and bombing all the way to Beirut.

3. Israel broke its promise when the IDF attacked Syrian forces without provocation on the very day that Prime Minister Begin announced in the Knesset that it would not fire on the Syrians without first being attacked.

4. Israel flagrantly disregarded its explicit contract commitment to America that it would use the weapons and equipment we provided exclusively for "self-defense"; instead it freely employed them to attack Lebanon and lay siege to West Beirut under circumstances that even Israelis admitted could not be justified as "self-defense".

5. Israel violated its contract with America that it would not use cluster bombs unless attacked by the "regular forces of a sovereign nation in which Israel is attacked by two or more of the nations Israel fought in 1967 and 1973" and that it would not in any event use such bombs "against any areas where civilians were exposed;" instead it used those bombs, in invading a neighboring country, to produce many civilian casualties.

6. Israel repeatedly violated cease-fire agreements arranged between June and August 1982.

7. As a part of the arrangements for the dispersal of the PLO leadership Israel pledged that the IDF would stay out of West Beirut; then, on September 15, 1982, in violation of that commitment, the IDF entered and refused to leave.

8. Israel betrayed America by flouting its promise to do nothing to jeopardize the safety of Palestinians left behind after the evacuation of the PLO leaders even though it knew that, in reliance on its assurance, America was pledging its own word. It let the notorious Phalange into the Sabra and Shatilla refugee camps where they massacred hundreds, if not thousands of Palestinian men, women, and children.

Errors by Israel

1. Israel erred when it annexed the Golan Heights in December 1981, thus assuring the undying enmity of Syria and laying the basis for a future war, since Israel's continued occupation of the Heights threatens Syria's security. By such annexation Israel made clear that it had no intention of ever agreeing to the demilitarization or internationalization of the Heights or exchanging them for peace, as contemplated by Resolution 242.

2. Israel erred by pursuing a settlements policy that not only directly violates the Geneva Convention of 1949 but, by preempting the land and water supplies of the West Bank, directly undercuts American policy. It reflects an Israeli decision to seek hegemony and war rather than peace.

3. Israel erred in believing that, by invading Lebanon and driving the PLO leadership out of Lebanon, it could destroy the PLO as a political force.

4. Israel erred in believing that it could gain a major influence in Lebanon by installing Bashir Gemayel as head of the Lebanese government, failing to recognize that

(a) the Maronites are too badly outnumbered to unify the country;

(b) the Druse and Shiite elements are too well armed and numerous to submit to Maronite domination; and

(c) Bashir—and later his brother Amin—would disappoint Israel by failing to commit the Phalange to assist Israel in taking control of Beirut, and refusing Israel the peace treaty that was one of the major objectives of its invasion.

5. Israel erred when it gratuitously attacked Syrian forces in the Bekaa Valley, exposing Syria's tactical inadequacies and systems inferiority. It thereby enabled Syria, with Soviet help, to rectify those deficiencies.

6. Israel erred when, in destroying the Syrian anti-aircraft missiles, it revealed tactics it had been developing for years; thus enabling Syria with Soviet help to develop counter measures.

7. Israel erred when, by disclosing the deficiencies in the Syrian army, it forced President Assad to speed the increase of Syria's armed forces to 400,000 active duty personnel. With the help of its new weapons and troops and 12,000 Soviet training personnel Syria has emerged substantially stronger than before in relation to Israel.

8. Israel erred when it humiliated a superpower, the Soviet Union, by revealing the inferiority of the weapons it had provided Syria, and thus compelling Moscow to re-equip Syria with advanced equipment and training personnel. Not only has this resulted in greatly enhancing Syria's military strength and thus diminishing Israel's balance of security, but it has enabled the Soviet Union to establish a substantial military presence (12,000 troops) in a key Middle Eastern country—a position it lost in 1974.

9. Israel erred in failing to recognize that no Maronite regime could grant it a peace treaty or even make the concessions provided in the May 17 agreement and still survive.

10. Israel erred during its occupation of the Chouf Mountains; because the IDF outraged the Druse by letting the Phalange enter and harass Druse villages, the Druse responded with a bloody massacre of the Maronites.

11. Israel erred fundamentally in pursuing hegemonic ambitions in Lebanon and elsewhere; such policies are imposing an intolerable burden on Israel's economy and finances while increasing, to an unhealthy degree, Israel's dependence on the United States diplomatically, militarily and economically.

12. Israel erred when it violated the cease-fire by sending the IDF into West Beirut; it erred tragically when the IDF opened the Sabra and Shatilla camps to the Phalange. That, in the phrase of Boulay de la Merthe, Fouché, Talleyrand—or whoever first said it—"was worse than a crime, it was a blunder."

13. Israel erred in invading Lebanon in futile pursuit of an unworkable scheme, since the result was to compel its Arab neighbors to build up their defenses and thus pose an increasing threat to Israel's survival.

Betrayals by the United States

1. Our government betrayed our commitment to the United Nations Charter

(a) when, having voted for a Security Council resolution condemning the Israeli annexation of the Golan Heights as illegal and calling for its revocation, it did nothing to enforce Israeli compliance;

(b) when it condemned Israel's use of American-supplied equipment for its aggressive attack on the Baghdad nuclear reactor yet continued furnishing arms for similar adventures; and

(c) when, on June 6, 1982, it voted for a Security Council resolution calling on Israel to stop its invasion of Lebanon and withdraw to its own borders without conditions, then not only vetoed the sanctions required to enforce the resolution but took no unilateral action to enforce it.

2. Our government further blotted its copy book when, a year later, it completely reversed its support in the United Nations for an unconditional Israeli withdrawal and undertook, with the personal intervention of the Secretary of State, to pressure the Gemayel government into granting Israel, as the price of the IDF's withdrawal, conditions that would seriously impair Lebanon's sovereignty.

3. Our government betrayed its principles as a humane nation when it allowed Israel to use cluster bombs against the civilian population of Lebanon yet applied no sanctions for their wilful misuse other than a brief suspension of shipments.

4. Our government betrayed the Palestinian families remaining after the evacuation of the PLO leaders by withdrawing our first contingent of Marines prematurely without making adequate arrangements to secure the safety of the Palestinians left behind, even though it promised the PLO leaders that it would "do its utmost".

5. Our government betrayed those thoughtful Israelis who are sensitive to the long-term implications of Israel's political and security predicament, view with dismay the prospective degeneration of their country into an aggressive, expansionist garrison state, and prefer a rational diplomacy to everlasting war. Had Washington expressed adequate opposition to Israel's aggression against Lebanon there is evidence that moderate Israeli elements in the government might well have prevented the invasion—or at least have stopped the IDF from besieging and entering Beirut, attacking Syria, and setting in train the events that led to the massacre of the Palestinian refugees in the Sabra and Shatilla camps and the death of our marines.

Postscript :
Israeli Efforts to Rewrite History

"Humankind", wrote T. S. Eliot, "cannot bear very much reality," and defeat is the bitterest of all realities. After the First World War, the Nazis and other right-wing elements in Germany invented the myth of the "stab in the back". The German army, they claimed, would have fought on to victory had the Social Democrats not undermined the home front by pacifism and defeatism. Since that myth had a profound effect on history it is not surprising that General Sharon should devise his own variation on the "stab in the back" theme to blame the United States for the failure of his Lebanese strategy. Nor is it surprising that his myth has gained currency with Israel's supporters; any individual or nation heavily dependent on another instinctively blames his or its patron for all failures and misfortunes, thus expressing the resentment that dependence engenders.

The Sharon Myth

Sharon's interpretation of the Lebanese adventure, enthusiastically echoed by some of Israel's friends in America, was that the IDF was on the verge of a glorious triumph when the United States snatched defeat from the jaws of victory. Since such a story appeals to connoisserus of bizarre explanations, the revisionists are now busily chiseling it into stone tablets for posterity. But, before it is accepted as handed down from Mount Sinai, it is well to take note of some inconvenient facts — which require a brief reconstruction of the actual fighting.

Sharon's story is a lament for what, he thought, might have been. In his version of fantasy history, the IDF was just about to deal Syria a humiliating defeat, when an ungrateful American government rushed in to impose a cease-fire that saved the Syrians. "Israel", according to Ariel Sharon, could not stand up against United States' pressure, although he tried to postpone the cease-fire for twenty-four hours because "with an additional few hours we would have cut off the Syrian army in the Beka'a in the area of Shtura, Zahle."[112]

But is that really true? Although it is not widely understood except by military critics, Israel found its attack on Syria unexpectedly heavy going; Syrian reinforcements had degraded Israel's combat advantage on terrain that was unfavorable to the attackers. Far from America's blowing the whistle that stopped an inevitable Israeli advance, Sharon and the Israeli cabinet moved unilaterally for a cease-fire because neither was prepared to pay the price for a

(*)This postscript was written largely by Dr. Douglas B. Ball, Lt. Col. M.S.C. (USAR)

138

larger victory. That appears in bold reflief from a hard look at military realities.[113]

What Really Happened in the Battle

The original campaign plan drawn up by the IDF seems to have differed materially from the one actually carried out. The original plan had provided that, on launching an invasion from the south, the IDF would simultaneously land forces on the enemy's rear; that move would have permitted the IDF to advance on Beirut and the Beirut-Damascus highway from two directions and would have blocked an enemy retreat.

But Sharon could not pursue that plan without having to disclose his full intentions to the Israeli cabinet and, since it might have tied his hands, he devised a more complicated strategy that called for three fronts and four routes of advance. On the western front, between the Mediterranean Sea and the Lebanon Mountains he deployed 35,000 troops backed by the Israeli Navy. The first column was to march along the coast road through Tyre, Sidon and Damour to Beirut. The second was to pick off the PLO strong point at Beaufort Castle, then push along the base of the Lebanon Mountains to cut the Beirut-Damascus Road near Ein Dara and encircle the Syrians in Beirut and in Behamdoun.

On the eastern front, 40,000 of the IDF were to advance in two columns up the Beka'a Valley to link up with the Beirut-Damascus highway around Shtura, a junction town, and Zahle, a Christian town presumably well disposed to Israel. That would open the way into upper Lebanon, thereby making it possible to drive the Syrians out of that region, should they fail to leave of their own volition.

In spite of ample warning, the Syrians and PLO had not disposed their forces wisely. In the East, a lone Syrian brigade was covering the entire Beka'a Valley from Hasbaniya to Karoun, while another brigade covered the SAM-6 missile sites along the Syrian frontier. The initial phase of the campaign in the East did not follow the Israeli scenario. The Syrian brigade was easily hustled out of its prepared positions near Hasbaniya and forced northward to Karoun, where on June 9th, the Syrian 1st Armored Division gave battle. Its efforts to check the IDF advance were greatly hindered by the superiority of its foe both on the ground and in the air, where the Israeli air force had already taken out the Syrian SAM-6 missiles and any Syrian planes that were unwise enough to enter the fray. Still, although badly outnumbered and lacking air cover, the Syrian line held until the afternoon when IDF units passed around the Syrian right flank at Lake Karoun, to destroy a brigade and over 150 Syrian tanks. The Syrians then retired in good order northward.

The Israelis followed up their success in a lethargic manner. Fuel shortages and the failure to press on during the night gave the Syrians precious time to dispatch the reinforcements that should have been in place weeks before. As a result, while the force operating on the slope of the Lebanese mountains, led by General Peled, made excellent, unopposed progress, the main advance walked into a Syrian ambush at Sultan Yakoub and had to beat a retreat. As a result, the Peled column, too far advanced and dangerously isolated, had to pull back two or three kilometers. That left the Israelis off the eastern side of the Beirut-Damascus Highway and eight kilometers from Shtura. The opportunity to capture these positions was not to come again, for by June 11th Syrian reinforcements were pouring in. In spite of heavy losses, Syrian armored strength had now risen from 100 to 500 tanks on the eastern front (there are today 1200). With nearly even numbers the combat ratio was no longer favorable even with air superiority; moreover a continuous front offered no chance for a flanking movement or other useful maneuvers. The prospect on June 11th was for a pitched battle which the Israelis chose to decline; instead they proposed a cease-fire.

Though thwarted in the east, Sharon later tried to achieve the same goal from the west. Here too conditions seemed propitious, for, if Syria's troops were poorly deployed in the east, their dispositions in the west left them badly exposed. Scattered about the countryside were the Syrian 85th Armored Brigade, together with two infantry brigades of the Palestine Liberation Army (PLA—under Syrian, not PLO control) supported by 15,000 PLO fighters. The IDF drove up the coast to within a few miles of Beirut, where they encountered the Syrians lying in ambush in Kefr Sil, on June 18th. Despite the dropping of leaflets urging the Syrians to leave Beirut while the road was still open, the Syrians refused to budge, and made every effort to assure that their line of communications with Damascus was kept open.

While these events were occurring on the coast, the second western column to which Sharon had assigned the major task of cutting off the Syrians, was delayed in traffic jams. It was not until June 7th, at Jezzin, that it encountered a Syrian armored brigade, backed by an infantry and a commando battalion. A hot all-day fight ensued with the badly outnumbered Syrians retiring under cover of night to Ein Dara, only three kilometers from the Beirut-Damascus Road.

Sharon's plan now depended for its success on the speed of the Israeli advance to capture the Damascus-Beirut highway. But the Israeli schedule was upset not so much by Syrian delaying actions but once again by fuel problems, which the exasperated commander, Menachem Einen, finally overcame by the remarkable expedient of refueling his tanks with gas requisitioned from a local service station.

Syrian resistance at Ein Zehalta (helped by French Gazelle anti-tank helicopters) wrecked Sharon's time table still further as did combat at Ein Dara. The latter engagement was still in progress when the Israelis on June 11th suddenly offered the Syrians (but not the PLO) a truce to which Syria agreed. Yet, as that truce did not hold, the Israelis availed themselves of the opportunity to improve their position and carry out their plans by driving the 85th Brigade, together with its supporting units, into Beirut and on June 14th linking up with the Christian enclave in East Beirut. On June 22-25, Sharon made a last attempt to capture Shtura. In 60 hours of hard fighting, the IDF tried to thwart any possibility of Syrian interference from Beirut by driving the Syrian units completely off the Beirut-Damascus Road, including at Shtura. He had only partially succeeded in that limited objective when the campaign came to a halt fully ten kilometers short of Shtura. Nor did Israel's eastern-front force, which was within range of the same goal, renew its efforts to assist the operation.

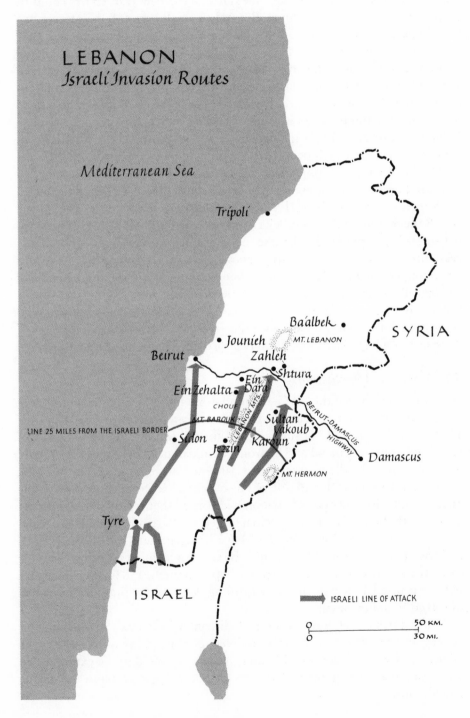

LEBANON
Israeli Invasion Routes

Mediterranean Sea

Tripoli •

Ba'albek •

SYRIA

• Jounieh   MT. LEBANON

Beirut •   Zahleh

Ein   •Shtura
Ein Zehalta •   Dara
CHOUF
MT. BAROUK   Sultan'
LINE 25 MILES FROM THE ISRAELI BORDER   Yakoub
• Sidon   Karoun
Jezzin   BEIRUT-DAMASCUS HIGHWAY

• Damascus

MT. HERMON

Tyre •

ISRAEL

▶ ISRAELI LINE OF ATTACK

0 ——————— 50 KM.
0 ——————— 30 MI.

The Actual Result

In spite of the fact that the supporters of Israel trumpeted a great and decisive victory, what had in fact happened? The Syrians had been mauled; they had been driven back, their missiles had been destroyed and their air force rendered ineffective until counter measures to the new IDF tactics could be prepared with Russian assistance. But only a small part of Syria's forces had been engaged and even those units had emphatically not been routed; they were able and willing to continue the fight and, although they had suffered heavy losses, they were far from beaten. The difference between the Israeli and the Syrian perceptions of these events paved the way for the ignominious end of the Lebanese adventure. By the time Israel realized that Syria had no intention of submitting to its show of force and abandoning its role in Lebanon, Russian aid had inflated the price in prospective casualties well above the level the Israeli people were willing to pay. As a result, it was Israel that had to abandon its objectives, not Syria.

Thus the facts make nonsense of Sharon's claim that, had the United States not forced a cease-fire, the IDF, "with an additional few hours...would have cut off the Syrian army in the Beka'a in the area of Shtura, Zahle." Throughout the sad history of the Lebanese incident, Sharon repeatedly ignored any cease-fires that did not serve his purposes. Those who argue that he would have stopped the fighting at a time when he thought himself on the verge of cutting off the enemy are either gullible or disingenuous. One can answer them only by repeating the words of the Duke of Wellington to a man who confronted him in Green Park with the greeting: "Mr. Robinson, I believe." To that the Duke replied: "Sir, if you believe that, you can believe anything."[114]

The Myth as Afterthought

In considering the validity of General Sharon's myth, it is important to note that, while the cease-fire he attributes to American pressure occurred on June 11, 1982, the myth did not surface until the fall of 1983. By then a series of catastrophes had occurred and Sharon was in bad need of a sacrificial villain. The Sabra and Shatilla massacres had darkened his reputation; our marines, the French and the IDF had suffered heavy casualties from truck bombs; the once friendly Shias of South Lebanon had turned that region into a shooting gallery with the IDF as their principal target; the Syrians had made clear that they would not leave Lebanon; the May 17th agreement had aborted; Israel had tried to play off the Druse against the Christians and was taking excessive casualties attempting to keep the peace between them, and finally, the dream of a centralized Lebanon run by a quisling Maronite regime in Beirut had dissolved in opium smoke.

Thus, during that bitter season of discontent General Sharon and his colleagues had every reason to try to divert public attention from their own failures and misjudgments by blaming America, which, to the extent it had any policy at all, was doing its best to secure Sharon's goals for him and paying Israel's bills.

America the Impotent

But if the military situation and the *ex post facto* invention of the myth cast doubts on the veracity of its inventors, just how much, if at all, was America responsible for slowing down Israel's effort to oust the Syrians? The June 11 unilateral cease-fire reflected the concern of the Israeli cabinet, including Prime Minister Begin, that the fighting was getting out of hand, and, in any event, the war did not stop; Israel continued its attacks from June 12 to June 14 and again from June 22 to June 25, when the IDF finally cut—then tried to clear—the Beirut-Damascus Highway. During that period, Prime Minister Begin, while visiting Washington, defiantly declared that America could not halt the IDF's drive even if it tried. He had, so he let it be known, cabled his Cabinet the day before telling them to take all needed action "regardless of these hints"—meaning presumably any American remonstrances.

So what about the cease-fires of June 11th, 14th and 25th? The Israelis rejected President Reagan's appeals for a cease-fire on June 9 and June 10 or so qualified them as to assure their rejection. When, on June 11, the Israeli cabinet announced a unilateral cease-fire for Syria only (not the PLO), Israeli leaders made it explicitly clear that that announcement was their own decision; indeed, the Israeli Foreign Minister, Yitzhak Shamir, indignantly denied that the action was taken at the behest of the Americans. When a *Washington Post* correspondent suggested that United States pressure may have triggered the cease-fire, a querulous Israeli official exclaimed "Why is it that every time we make a decision to try to calm the situation, it has to be the result of pressure from the Americans?"[115]

Still that will not stop Israel's American apologists from repeating the myth; for, needing a scapegoat who won't answer back, they blame Israeli mistakes on America by conditioned reflex. It will certainly not deter Mr. William Safire, for example, from continuing to write that when President Reagan "ordered the Israelis to stop winning" he committed "a blunder comparable only to Eisenhower's Suez mistake in 1956", since, writes Safire, he accepted the assumption "abetted by the State Department's Philip Habib" that "the problem would be to get the Israelis, not the Syrians, out of Lebanon."[116] And no doubt the American Jewish Committee's magazine, *Commentary*, will continue to publish articles, such as a recent one by Michael Ledeen, where it is asserted that "Washington acted to halt the Israeli advance just when a decisive military victory was within days or even hours of achievement."[117]

Finally, there will be no deterring the indefatigable Norman Podhoretz, the editor of *Commentary*, from continuing to castigate President Reagan because "Far from cheering the Israelis on when they went to war against Soviet-backed armies in Lebanon, Mr. Reagan kept pressing for a cease-fire. Then, having sent in a contingent of United States Marines, not to fight but to keep the peace, he withdrew them as soon as they came under serious attack. And having promised to retaliate against Syria for this attack, he no more did so than Mr. Carter before him retaliated against Iran."[118]

Thus is history shamelessly rewritten.

Notes

PART ONE

1. American forces briefly entered Lebanon from July to October 1958 to help ease President Camille Chamoun out of office and replace him with General Fuad Shehab who was more generally acceptable and who was ready to promote needed reforms. But the groundwork for that change had been laid before the troops arrived and the *terminus ad quem* was already known.
   Facts on File Yearbook 1958. Vol. XVIII, New York, 1959. pp. 162-3, 322, 347.

2. Civil and military aid to Israel in 1946-74 was as follows:

Loans	$2,946.8 million
Grants	1,678.5 million
Total Aid	$4,625.3 million

   Civil and military aid to Israel in 1975-81 was as follows:

Loans	$ 7,687.0 million
Grants	8,371.9 million
Total Aid	$16,028.9 million

   $2,270.8 million of loans have been repaid with interest from earlier grants and approximately $7,000 million of new aid and grants (with forgiveness of debts) occurred in fiscal years 1982 and 1983. One might have expected that Israel's defense expenditures would decline after Egypt, its strongest opponent, made peace, but in fact, they have increased.
   U.S. Overseas Loans & Grants Obligations and Loan Authorizations. July 1, 1945 to September 30, 1981. U.S. Bureau of the Budget, Washington, D.C. 1982. pp. 18, 28.

3. The Arms Export Control Act, 22 USC Sec. 3201, 3302; also the U.S. Foreign Assistance Act of 1961 as amended.

4. Congress cut off aid effective February 5, 1975 in the Foreign Aid Bill passed in 1974. When Turkey did not withdraw from Cyprus, the cut-off went into effect and, with the exception of a small grant in 1977, was not rescinded until April 1978.

5. "Secret" memorandum for the President from Walter B. Smith, dated October 21, 1953, Box 10, folder Israeli Relations 1951-7, Dulles Papers. Subject Series, Dwight D. Eisenhower Presidential Library, declassified August 31, 1981. On this occasion Eisenhower ordered the Treasury not to issue a $16 million aid check until Israel cooperated with the United Nations by discontinuing its efforts to effect the unilateral diversion of Jordan River water at B'not Yaakov — a diversion that would violate the armistice agreement between Syria and Israel since that diversion would adversely affect both Syria and Jordan. Not only did President Eisenhower halt economic aid until Israel cooperated, he also instructed the Treasury Department to draft an order removing the tax deductible status of contributions made to the United Jewish Appeal and to other Zionist organizations raising private funds for Israel in America.
   Stephen Green, *Taking Sides: America's Secret Relations with a Militant Israel,* (New York: William Morrow & Company, 1984). p. 80.
   The President's action produced the desired result; Israel stopped work on the canal.
   Again, on October 31, 1956 Eisenhower terminated all American aid when Israel invaded Egypt in connection with the Suez affair. Then, having established that his word should be taken seriously, he effectively used the threat of an aid cut-off to force Israel to comply with a United Nations resolution and withdraw from Gaza over Ben-Gurion's clamorous resistance.
   Townsend Hoopes, *The Devil and John Foster Dulles,* Atlantic Little Brown, 1973, pp. 390, 391; Peter Grose, *Israel in the Mind of America,* Knopf, 1983, p. 304. For the text of the Eisenhower speech of February 2, 1957 see *The Arab-Israel Conflict,* edited by John Norton Moore, Princeton University Press, 1977, pp. 1011, 1017.

Today one can scan the political horizon without finding anyone in either party with the fortitude to follow Eisenhower's incisive precedent. As a result some have contended that, since no President will enforce America's contract rights — nor will Congress support him if he tries — we should eliminate restrictions on Israel's use of our military and economic aid and stop being sanctimonious about it. It is quite unconscionable for us to enforce our contract rights against Turkey and ignore them with regard to Israel.

6. On the basis of past experience with Israel, Senator Mark O. Hatfield has expressed doubt as to the usefulness of those restrictions. Although he explicitly recognizes that the interests of the United States and Israel are by no means fully congruent — a point that will be developed later in this book — he contends that "once the United States delivers weapons to another nation, we cannot reasonably expect to control the use of those weapons. Control exists only prior to delivery", he says, "and it is dangerously foolish to suppose otherwise. The threat of holdups in future deliveries is not likely to deter a nation already engaged in a war, particularly when history indicates that such delays are never more than temporary."

So far as Israel is concerned, history has born out Senator Hatfield's comments. But that is largely because recent Presidents have never seriously stopped the flow of aid to Israel as America did in the case of Turkey; thus Israeli governments feel free to disregard our threats. Had recent American governments shown the courage to enforce America's contract rights against Israel — or were our current government to do so now — the threat of such sanctions would have real meaning.

Those who advocate eliminating contractural restrictions should carefully consider what such a decision implies. If Senator Hatfield is right that "control exists only prior to delivery" of weapons and that the recipient nation will freely use those weapons for its own purposes, then we should, in advance of delivery, severely limit the quantity and character of the military weapons and equipment we provide, restricting such aid rigorously to the minimum necessary to assure Israel's "legitimate self-defense". By no means should we continue to maintain Israel as the fourth strongest military power in the world — which it claims to be today — since Israeli governments show little inclination to take account of America's interests, while exhibiting a strong drive to expand Israeli territory.

That position is essential if America is to maintain any policy of its own in the Middle East and not continue — as has lately been the case — to serve as the mere subject — and sometimes the victim — of Israeli ambitions.

7. Amnon Kapeliuk, 'Begin and the 'Beasts' ", *New Statesman*, June 25, 1982, reprinted in *Israeli Invasion of Lebanon, Press Profile June/July 1982.* Claremont Research and Publications, August 1982. p. 93. Also; Noam Chomsky, *The Fateful Triangle*, (Boston: South End Press, 1983.) pp. 198-201; *The Washington Post*, July 15, 1982.

8. *Ha'aretz*, June 25, 1982.

9. Henry Kamin, *The New York Times*, July 11, 1982.

10. The official Kahan Report, made after the Sabra and Shatilla killings, describes the Phalangists' view of the matter. The report states that "the subject of the Palestinian population in Lebanon, from among whom the terrorist operations sprang up and in the midst of whom their military infrastructure was entrenched, came up more than once in meetings between Phalangist leaders and Israeli representatives. The position of the Phalangist leaders . . . was, in general, that no unified and independent Lebanese state could be established without a solution being found to the problem of the Palestinian refugees, who, according to the Phalangist estimates, numbered half a million people. In the opinion of the Phalangists, that number of refugees, for the most part Moslems, endangered the demographic balance between the Christian and Moslems in Lebanon . . . and the stability of the state of Lebanon and the status of the Christians in that country. Therefore, the Phalangist leaders proposed removing a large portion of the Palestinian refugees from Lebanese soil, whether by methods of persuasion or other means of pressure. They did not conceal their opinion that it would be necessary to resort to acts of violence in order to cause the exodus of many Palestinian refugees from Lebanon." The report contains no evidence that the Israeli representatives dissented from this view or made any serious effort to dissuade the Phalangists from carrying out the policy they outlined.

Kahan Report, as quoted in *The Israeli Invasion of Lebanon Part II. Press Profile: August 1982/May 1983.* Claremont Research and Publications, New York. 1983. p. 205.

11. Ze'ev Schiff, *Ha'aretz*. May 23. 1982.

12. Yoel Marcus, "The War is Inevitable" *Ha'aretz*. May 23, 1982.

13. Benny Morris, "Diligent Diarist", (Review of David Ben-Gurion's Diaries) *The Jerusalem Post*, (International edition), April 22-28, 1984. p. 19.

14. Livia Rokach, *Israel's Sacred Terrorism*, (AAUG Information Paper Series; No. 23, 1980) pp. 24-30. Bashir Gemayel originally approached the Israelis for help against the Syrians. The history of the discussions that followed is contained in Schiff and Ya'ari, *Israel's Lebanon War* (New York: Simon and Schuster, 1984) pp. 31-61.

15. *Time*, February 15, 1982. p. 80.

16. Israeli leaders saw that zone as useful not only for its defense but also for facilitating its plans to divert Lebanon's water resources to its own depleting aquifers.

17. Ze'ev Schiff, "Green Light, Lebanon", *Foreign Policy*, Spring 1983.
    This plan had been hatched in discussions over a long number of years. The background is described in Jonathan C. Randal, *Going All the Way*. (New York: Viking Press, 1983.)

18. "Israel's Strategic Problems in the Eighties", an address by Defense Minister Ariel Sharon, prepared for delivery at a conference of the Institute of Strategic Studies, Tel Aviv University, December 14, 1981, and published as a press bulletin dated Jerusalem, December 15, 1981.

19. How much this statement was inspired by naivete and how much by domestic politics is anyone's guess. President Reagan evidently had not learned the lesson implied by Secretary Haig's ill-fated venture in alliance building in the Middle East in early 1981. When Haig asked the moderate Arab states to join the United States and Israel in the defense of the Gulf against the Soviet menace, the Arab leaders replied (a) The Soviets were not a serious, immediate threat to their security; (b) Israel was; (c) They would resist having Israeli troops on their soil regardless of the circumstances; and (d) No security arrangements as proposed could be agreed to until there was a comprehensive peace with Israel, which must include the Palestinians.

20. *Facts on File 1981*. p. 489 2E. A suspension lasted only a few days. There was a short suspension after the Iraq reactor bombing in June 1981, but shipments were soon resumed and, although the U.S. joined in the Security Council Resolution to condemn the annexation of the Golan Heights, the United States vetoed a resolution to impose sanctions on Israel.

21. *Facts on File 1982*. (New York: Facts on File, Inc., 1982) p. 34 G2 (January 20)

22. The quotations on this and following pages are from: Alexander M. Haig, Jr., *Caveat: Realism, Reagan, and Foreign Policy*. (New York: Macmillan Publishing Company, 1984.) pp. 323, 326, 330, 333, 334, 335.

23. Ze'ev Schiff and Ehud Ya'ari, *Israel's Lebanon War* (Edited and Translated by Ina Friedman). (New York: Simon and Schuster, 1984.) pp. 31. The authors report that when Begin made a trip to Washington during the second week of the war the White House was known to be unhappy that the IDF had entered Beirut. Still Haig insisted on arranging a visit between Begin and the President, advising Begin in advance of the meeting, "Hold out for what you want." As the meeting concluded and the participants took their leave, Haig was seen to give Begin a surreptitious thumbs up sign. (p. 202)

24. Very few PLO personnel were killed on these occasions. Since the PLO leadership had learned not to stay more than twelve hours in any one place it was generally innocent and unknowing neighbors who were killed. PLO offices under these circumstances consisted of a telephone, a few chairs, tables and a filing cabinet. *Facts on File 1982*. p. 414 C2 (June 11).

25. Schiff and Ya'ari, *op. cit.*, p. 98.

26. Between 1945 and 1970, the United States, as a matter of policy, scrupulously refrained from using its veto power to block Security Council Resolutions; during that same period, the Soviet Union used its veto 103 times. Since 1970, however, the situation has changed drastically, with the United States casting 38 vetoes and the Soviet Union casting only 9. All but four United States vetoes related to three topics: Israel-Palestine 15; South Africa-Namibia 14; Vietnam 5. Vetoes were cast by successive administrations as follows: Nixon 4; Ford 14; Carter 4; and Reagan 16. Thus, under the Reagan Administration we have averaged four vetoes a year.
    The United States was joined by Britain and France (or, on four occasions, by Britain alone) in casting 13 of those vetoes; with respect to the remaining 25 it stood alone. More than half of its lonely vetoes resulted when the United States was single-handedly defending Israel from either censure or sanctions.
    Official Information Sheet furnished by the US Mission to the United Nations on May 9, 1984.

27. Haig, *op. cit.,* pp. 338, 339, 341.

28. *Facts on File 1982.* p. 414 2B to 3B. A high Israeli military aide later admitted to Washington reporters on June 29 that Israel's stated goal had been "perhaps misleading".

29. *Time.* February 15, 1982. p. 80.

30. Ze'ev Schiff, "Green Light, Lebanon". *Foreign Policy.* Spring 1983. pp. 73-85.

31. *Facts on File 1982.* p. 558 (August 6).
The Adminstration allegedly sent a list of military, economic, and diplomatic sanctions that would be *considered* if Israel continued its attack.

32. *The New York Times.* July 15, 1982. Paul L. Montgomery quoting Leonard Fein, editor of *Moment* magazine.
Even this appraisal was an understatement, for the rubric of "self defense" can scarcely be stretched to justify the preemptive attack on the Sinai and the Suez Canal in 1956 or the Israeli invasion of Lebanon in 1978. Prime Minister Begin told the National Defense College in Jerusalem on August 8, 1982, that Israel had fought only three of its wars "without an alternative." One was the war of independence which lasted from 1947 to 1949; the second was the war of attrition that preceded the Yom Kippur War; and the third was the Yom Kippur War. In its Sinai campaign against Egypt in 1956, Israel, he said, "had a choice"; the purpose of that war was to "destroy the fedayeen, who did not represent a danger to the state." It "again had a choice" in the six-day war in 1967. "The Egyptian Army concentrations in the Sinai approaches do not prove that Nasser was really about to attack us. Let us be truthful with ourselves. Nasser did not attack us. We decided to attack him." Nor, said Begin, did the invasion of Lebanon, which he called the "Operation Peace for Galilee", ". . . really belong to the category of wars of no alternative."
Quoted in G. H. Jansen, "The Shattered Myths", *Middle East International.* 18 February 1983 p. 13.

33. Ze'ev Schiff, "Green Light in Lebanon", *Foreign Policy,* Spring 1983. p. 79.

34. Schiff and Ya'ari, *op. cit.,* pp. 112, 113.

35. *Ibid.,* p. 152.

36. Haig, *op. cit.,* p. 340.

37. *Ibid.,* p. 341.

38. Schiff and Ya'ari, *op. cit.,* p. 229.

39. *Newsweek.* February 20, 1984. p. 47.

40. Schiff and Ya'ari, *op. cit.,* p. 225.

41. *Facts on File 1982.* p. 583 2F (August 13)

42. *Facts on File 1982.* p. 348 2D (June 25)
Begin's stormy meeting with U.S. Congressmen and Senators was in marked contrast with the cordial reception he had received at the White House the day before (June 20, 1982). Evidently the President did not share the concerns felt on Capital Hill or had not been adequately briefed.

43. Robert Fisk, *The Times,* (London), October 7, 1982. p. 32.

44. *The New York Times,* October 12, 1982.

45. William Espinoza, *Defense or Aggression,* American Educational Trust. Washington, D.C., pp. 15, 16.

46. *T. Elaine Carey, The Christian Science Monitor,* August 19, 1982.
Warren Richey, *The Christian Science Monitor,* November 2. 1982.

47. *The Chistian Science Monitor,* July 21, 1982, p. 2.

48. Report of the Subcommittee of the Committee on Armed Services, House of Representatives, 98th Congress, First Session, entitled "Adequacy of U.S. Marine Corps Security in Beirut", p. 25.

49. *The New York Times,* July 8, 1982; text of Tass announcement on p. A6.

50. With a more sophisticated sense of maneuver, the Adminstration might have used this opportunity to stengthen America's position in the Middle East (the Arab states and the Soviet Union were willing to do nothing) by ignoring its self-denying ordinance not to deal with the PLO. Appropriately safeguarded negotiations might have produced a settlement. In any case, for a brief moment, Secretary of State George P. Shultz, during his Senate confirmation hearings, recognized that there was a direct connection between peace and a solution to the legitimate needs and desires of the Palestinian people.

51. Schiff and Ya'ari, *op. cit.,* p. 251.

52. PORI public opinion polls discussed in *Yediot Aharonot,* August 6, 1982;
    Ha'aretz, November 18, and December 27, 1982.

53. "Reagan's Lebanon Policy: Trial and Error", *The Middle East Journal,* Spring 1984, p. 239.

54. Not all Israelis perceived the origins of the Plan in the same light as William Quandt. Meron Benvenisti, the former Deputy Mayor of Jerusalem, suggests in a recent study of the West Bank problem that the proposal was essentially an act of expiation. "When the true aim of the war became clear and the new Palestinian tragedy was revealed in its full horror, the United States attempted to clear itself of all blame by publishing the Reagan initiative."
    "The West Bank Data Project—A Survey of Israel's Policies"; American Enterprise Institute for Public Policy Research, 1984, Washington, D.C.

55. William Quandt, *op. cit.,* p. 239.

56. *Facts on File 1982.* p. 658 H4 (September 10)
    Israel also postponed the autonomy talks with Egypt and Shamir noted that, had Israel known of the U.S. plans, peace would not have been concluded with Egypt.

57. All this was strictly illegal. *DA PAM 27-1 Treaties Governing Land Warfare—December 1956.* p. 150. The last paragraph of Article 49 of the Geneva Convention Relative to the Protection of Civilian Persons in Time of War, 12 August 1949, reads: "The Occupying Power shall not deport or transfer parts of its own civilian population into the territory it occupies." This clause was inserted after World War II because of Nazi abuses in Poland and elsewhere. The same convention protects civilians whether the occupying state annexes the occupied area or not (article 47). Article 53 further forbids the destruction of private or state property "except where such destruction is rendered absolutely necessary by military operations." Houses from which suspected resistance has been offered have been regularly demolished by the Israeli occupying authorities.

58. *Facts on File 1984.* pp. 156-7, (March 2, 1984).

59. Milton Viorst, "America's Broken Pledge to the PLO", *The Washington Post,* December 19, 1982; see also Noam Chomsky *op. cit.* pp. 388, 389.

60. Loren Jenkins, "Israelis Hunt Palestinian Sympathizers in Beirut", *The Washington Post,* September 18, 1982. See also Chaim Herzog, *The Arab-Israeli Wars* (New York: Vintage Books, 1984) p. 352.

61. Chomsky, *op. cit.* p. 388.

62. Bernard Gwertzman, *The New York Times,* September 17, 1982, p. 1.

63. *The Commission of Inquiry into the Events at the Refugee Camps in Beirut—1983—Final Report* (Kahan Report). Reprinted in *The Israeli Invasion of Lebanon: Part II, Press Profile, August 1982-May 1983,* p. 206, Column 2. The most notorious massacre was that at Tel Za'atar Camp in August 1976 when the Phalange murdered thousands of Palesinians in revenge for a massacre of thousands of Christians in Damour in January of 1976.

64. PORI public opinion polls discussed in *Yediot Aharonot,* August 6, 1982; *Ha'aretz,* November 18 and December 27, 1982.

65. Daniel Gavron, *Israel After Begin,* (Boston: Houghton Mifflin Co., 1984 p. 117.

66. *Ibid.,* pp. 118-119.

67. Bernard Gwertzman, "U.S. Presses Israel to let U.N. Troops Move into Beirut", *The New York Times*, September 19, 1982, p. 1.

68. They were denounced by Arafat for *not* resisting the Israelis, thereby incurring, in true peacekeeping tradition, enemies on *both* sides.

69. Press conference, 28 September 1982. *Facts on File.* p. 715. 1C.

70. Randal, *op. cit.* p. 10. Gemayel later found it prudent to deny any meeting with the Israelis or that he accepted any of their terms. *Facts on File*, September 10, 1982. p. 659.

71. Schiff and Ya'ari, *op. cit.,* 233.

72. *Ibid.,* p. 287-288.

73. Nahum Barnea, *Koteret Rashit,* May 11, 1983. "Last Friday, the government ratified an agreement while hoping that it would never be put into practice. It was Begin who planted this hope in the hearts of his ministers. . . . Syria is supposed now to save Israel from an agreement it cannot live with. As the cabinet secretary explained after the meeting, the government's capitulation to US pressure was not designed to pave the way for an agreement with another Arab country but to improve our relations with the United States, which had greatly deteriorated." Reprinted in *The Israeli Invasion of Lebanon: Part II Press Profile: August 1982/May 1983.* 352.

74. *Facts on File 1983,* pp. 357-359. (May 20) Arab supporters of the agreement and the Lebanese parliament in its vague resolution all talked of restoring Lebanese sovereignty over its territory. When the terms confirmed that Israel was to have joint patrols in southern Lebanon, that Major Haddad was to continue to play a role, that the agreement terminated the state of war between the two countries and thus amounted to an Arab recognition of Israel, and that there were secret understandings with the United States, opposition mounted instantly. Saudi Arabia fell silent, the National Salvation Front was organized with Syria's blessing and support and Lebanon's borders were closed to cut off the possible flow of disguised Israeli goods to other parts of the Arab world, a move calculated to ruin Lebanon's economy as an entrepot.

75. Claudia Wright, "All Systems Stop", *Middle East International,* May 27, 1983. pp. 3-4.

76. Haddad, "Divided Lebanon", *Current History,* January 1982. p. 34.

77. Immediately after the May 17 Agreement, attacks on Israeli soldiers began in the occupied zone. The number of Israeli dead (368 in October 1982) rose to over 490 by June 1, 1983 and 586 by June 1, 1984. As an Israeli officer put it *(Time,* June 13, 1983, p. 44) "now they shoot at anything that looks Israeli." Begin then had to pledge in the Knesset that he would "bring our sons home from Lebanon." Simultaneously, violence in the West Bank and Gaza Strip increased ominously; "terrorist" attacks were up 69% to 110 and street demonstrations from 2,467 to 4,417, which suggested that removal of the PLO from Lebanon had done the Israelis little good. *Facts on File 1983.* p. 425, (June 10).

78. *The Israeli Invasion of Lebanon: Part II Press Profile: August 1982/May 1983.* (Claremont Research and Publishing, NYC) pp. 171-173.

79. *Middle East International.* August 19, 1983. p. 34. Jim Muir, "The Knives at Gemayel's Throat."

80. *Facts on File.* September 2, 1983. p. 662.

81. *Ibid.* September 16, 1983. pp. 698-699. While this may have been a correct interpretation of events at the time, the Administration had a strong incentive to put the best face on affairs it could, since the Democrats in Congress were trying to invoke the War Powers Act. There is no doubt that later shellings were direct expressions of Druse and Shiite disapprobation of our conduct. The Italians, who kept out of the local quarrels, suffered only a handful of fatalities.

82. During the Egyptian-Israeli War of Attrition in 1970, a United Nations force came under such continued heavy fire with resulting casualties that General Bull ordered their withdrawal from what he termed a "shooting gallery." There are other similar precedents.

83. The Administratin never could seem to make up its mind why it was firing those guns. One day it was to protect the marines (the pretext best likely to sit well with Congress). The next day it was to support the Lebanese Government, thereby associating ourselves with the Gemayel regime's attempt to control Lebanon, not the usual function of a peacekeeping force. The confusion reached its height

in February 1984, when the Secretary of the Navy, John Lehman, announced one morning that we were shelling Druse positions to support Gemayel and then corrected himself that afternoon, at White House insistence, to say we were protecting the marines. Since the Secretary had presumably based his morning statement on guidance furnished by the Administration, one wonders who was in charge. *Facts on File.* February 10, 1983. p. 82.

84. *Ibid.* October 28, 1983. pp. 818-9. The complete Reagan text is quoted.

85. *Ibid.* September 30, 1983. p. 738.

86. Except in the sense that the President named the MX Missile the "peacekeeper". During frontier days the Colt .45 was called a "peacemaker", and a cannon bearing that same name blew up in 1844, killing the Tyler Administration's Secretary of State and Secretary of the Navy. Euphemisms can be dangerous to the health.

87. Car bombs had been a standard mode of murder by all factions in Lebanon for years. *Facts on File 1983.* p. 679. (August 26).

88. *Ibid.* October 26, 1983. pp. 809, 813-4.

89. Thus, in spite of the IRA's bloody provocations, the British have been true to their own traditions. Had they followed Israel's precedent they might have reacted to the bombing of Harrod's, for example, by a mass destruction of the Catholic neighborhoods of Belfast — or, faithfully imitating the Israelis in Lebanon, they might have invaded the Irish Republic and bombed Dublin because some IRA operatives are known to be hiding there.

90. Henry A. Kissinger. *Years of Upheaval.* (Boston: Little, Brown & Co., 1982), p. 1075. Assad's independence was further demonstrated by his refusal — against Soviet urgings — to call off those Palestinians who were attacking Arafat in Lebanon.

91. *Facts on File 1983.* pp. 901-2, (December 2). Another underlying reason for the agreement may have been Secretary Shultz's desire to get back at Syria for embarrassing him and also to apply pressure on Assad. But Assad was in a strong tactical posture. The Israelis were not eager for another war — particularly since the Syrians had now established newly prepared and rearmed positions — and the United States Congress was already restive about marine casualties. In order to win, Assad needed only to consolidate his hold over Lebanon and wait. *The Jerusalem Post* (International Edition), David Bernstein, "Gemayel on the Syrian Bandwagon", March 4-10, 1984, pp. 14-15.

PART TWO

92. *Newsweek,* February 20, 1984, p. 47.

93. Donald Neff, *Warriors for Jerusalem.* (New York: Linden Press/Simon & Schuster, 1984.) p. 352.

94. "U.S. Assistance to the State of Israel", Uncensored Draft Report of the U.S. General Accounting Office. (1984). Appendices 3, 4, 5. pp. 15-17. *U.S. Overseas Loans and Grants.* Office of Planning and Budgeting, Bureau for Program and Policy Coordination, Agency for International Development, Vol. 1977 p. 19; Vol. 1981. p. 18.

95. Richard R. F. Sheehan. *The Arabs, Israelis, and Kissinger.* (New York: Readers Digest Press, 1976.) p. 199.

96. Henry Kissinger, *A World Restored.* (New York: University Library, 1964.) p. 2.

97. *The New York Times,* March 14, 1984. p. 1.
   Also: *CBS: Face the Nation,* March 18, 1984.

98. Philip Geyelin, "Why King Hussein Blew His Stack". *The Washington Post,* March 21, 1984.

99. *Ma'ariv,* January 3, 1984. For examples of such expansionist rhetoric see also *The Jerusalem Post* (International Edition), June 3-10, 1984, pp. 12, 14, 15, etc. where expulsion of the Arabs from the land of Israel and the need to extend Israeli rule to over 50,000 square miles of Arab-ruled lands is

openly discussed as a desirable and even feasible policy. See: *Middle East International,* Yezid Sayigh. "If Syria and Israel Should Fight It Out." No. 201, May 27, 1983, pp. 10-11.

100. Gary Putka, *The Wall Street Journal,* August 3, 1984, p. 20.

101. See the following sources of this table:

Stephen Green, *op. cit.* pp. 68, 98. *Britannica Book of the Year 1957,* pp. 122-3. *Britannica Book of the Year 1968,* p. 269; *The Military Balance.* International Institute for Strategic Studies. 1973. pp. 31-37; *The Military Balance.* International Institute for Strategic Studies. 1983-4; pp. 52-65. The Jordanian National Consultative Council has passed a decree calling for a "Peoples Army" on the Iraqi model of 200,000 men and women. *Middle East International.* No. 202, June 10, 1983, p. 6.

102. It is estimated that approximately 500,000 Israeli citizens live outside Israel to avoid its harsh taxes and repetitive demands for military service. Over 350,000 of these are reported to live within a 50 mile radius of New York City. Such absenteeism undermines the economy, increases the need for aid and requires those who are left to bear heavier service duties.

103. Anthony H. Cordesman, *The Gulf and the Search for Strategic Stability.* (Boulder: Westview Press, Inc., 1984) p. 973. For emigration figures see sources cited in Cordesman, *op. cit.,* p. 97.

104. It is to be noted that the United States Command and General Staff School at Leavenworth has long had a series of war gaming problems centered around "Dromar" (Israel) which assumes that Jordan and Israel are under one government and friendly to the United States; that Opforia (Syria) will be the party with whom a United States light corps will be engaged and that Saudi Arabia will be a hostile neutral. Iraq is left out of the play. In spite of the supposed need to protect the oil regions, the war is strictly an Israel vs. Syrian affair. Perhaps in Lebanon our officers, remembering their school problems, thought we would speedily rout Syria as in the game scenario. If so, the Syrians failed to play by the rules.

105. Cordesman, *op. cit.,* pp. 978, 979.

106. *The New York Times.* December 3, 1974, p. 11; December 4, 1974, p. 14; Also: *Al Roy.* Horizon Press, 1975, p. 169.

107. The value of the Israeli Pound has been as follows: The shekel which replaced it is worth ten times more.

Date	Value
1948	$2.80
1956	.60
1967	.32
1973	.23
1984	.00025 (1/40 cent)

When Begin on July 17, 1983 came up with his patronizing scheme of an economic union and technical aid proposal for Jordan, the Jordanians not only styled it "ridiculous"—they countered with a proposal to send a technical mission of their own to Israel to assist Begin in reordering Israel's finances! Source: *Britannica Year Book,* Israel articles for the years cited plus recent newspaper reports.

108.

ISRAELI TRADE FIGURES
(millions of dollars)

Date	Exports	Imports	Deficit
1975	$1,941	$4,173	$2,232
1980	5,538	8,027	2,489
1981	5,670	7,993	2,323
1982	5,282	8,116	2,834
1984			5,200 est.

Statistical Abstract of Israel 1982.

109. William Claiborne. "Israel Moves to Smooth Ties With the United States After Golan Action". *The Washington Post,* December 15, 1981.

110. General Brown's remarks are quoted in *Facts on File,* October 13, 1976, pp. 787 C1-G1;

111. Cordesman, *op. cit.*, p. 979.

POSTSCRIPT

112. David K. Shipler, "Scorn for U.S. in Israel", *The New York Times*, March 1, 1984, p. A10.

113. The reconstruction of the fighting is based largely on the *The New York Times*, June 7-23, 1982; Chaim Herzog, *The Arab-Israeli Wars* (New York: Vintage Books, 1984), pp. 392-351; Albert Bourge and Pierre Weiss, *Liban.* Editions Published. Paris 1983; Schiff and Ya'ari, *op. cit.*, pp. 109-131; 151-180.

114. Richard Aldington. *The Duke,* (New York: Garden City Publishing Company, 1943.) p. 364.

115. *Facts on File.* June 18, 1982, p. 432-2D.

116. *The New York Times*, September 25, 1983. Also *The New York Times*, June 11, 1984. p. A19.

117. Michael Ledeen, "The Lessons of Lebanon". *Commentary.* New York, May 1984, p. 17.

118. Norman Podhoretz, "Reagan, Man of Peace", *The New York Times*, June 13, 1984.

Index